CRITICAL ACCLAIM FOR JACKIE TORRENCE AND HER GREAT AMERICAN STORIES:

"One of the country's most honored storytellers."
—Southern Magazine

"Audiences all over the United States gather to hear her stories and to watch the exuberant teller."
—Woman's World

"She can flash her eyes open and shut faster than a spooked owl, jiggle all over like a bashful bear and weave a gossamer web of breath-holding suspense."
—The Christian Science Monitor

"Ms. Torrence enthralls kids and adults."
—Wall Street Journal

"A dazzling storyteller."
—Philip Morris Magazine

THE IMPORTANCE OF POT LIQUOR

JACKIE TORRENCE

St. Martin's Paperbacks

Published by arrangement with August House, Inc.

THE IMPORTANCE OF POT LIQUOR

Library of Congress Catalog Card Number: 94-9746

ISBN: 0-312-95688-6

Printed in the United States of America

August House hardcover edition published 1994
St. Martin's Paperbacks edition/December 1995

St. Martin's Paperbacks are published by St. Martin's Press, 175 Fifth Avenue, New York, N.Y. 10010.

10 9 8 7 6 5 4 3 2 1

To Lori
who is my lifelong inspiration

and Mrs. Sue Harvey
who gave me the title of this book
in a restaurant on an April morning
in Demopolis, Alabama.

Contents

THE MAP OF

UNCLE SAMPSON & AUNT MAG'S HOUSE

PLOW FIELDS

ROSE BUSHES

BIG DITCH

APPLE TREE

AUNT SALLY'S HOUSE

MINT

SALLY'S BARN

ROOT CELLAR

MINT

FOOT PATH

BIG RIVER ROCK GARDEN

WELL

SALLY'S OUTHOUSE

UNCLE FRED'S BASKET YARD

NARCISSUS IRIS

HALL MAPLE

JOHN WILSON'S PIG PEN

BIG GULLY

ROAD ENDS

SECOND CREEK

CARSON TOWN ROAD

LOCK HUFFMAN'S LAND

BLACK BERRY BRIARS

CRAB APPLE

FOOT PATH

PEAR TREE

SAGE

COTTON WOOD

TULIPS & DAFFODILS

BARN

SHEDS

HALL MAPLE

PEACH TREES

GRANDMA & GRANDPA'S HOUSE

RAIN BARREL

CHICKEN HOUSE

MINT

MINT

MILK PIT

MUSCADINE ARBOR

CATNIP PATCH

WELL

GRANDPA'S GARDEN

OUTHOUSE

THE IMPORTANCE OF POT LIQUOR

The Importance
of Pot Liquor

This story of pot liquor has its beginnings in slavery. Now, the whole system of slavery was arranged this way: the strong women and men were made to work the fields, and the women were also used to produce big strong babies for sale and trade. There were also yard slaves and kitchen slaves. The cook was usually a slave who had been on the plantation a long while and was entrusted with the management of the kitchen, the house, and the house slaves.

The working plantation was often the site for large gatherings. The master and his wife were entertainers. They entertained the neighbors from nearby plantations and, of course, relatives, visiting friends, merchants, and tradesmen.

After a feast was held, there was much cleaning

to be done. Pots, pans, and dishes had to be washed and put away. What food remained was used to feed the slaves. The big pot that had been used to cook turnip, mustard, or collard greens had gallons of left-over seasoned liquid. This was called pot liquor.

Now, this pot liquor was not thrown away but simply added to other pot liquor from meat and beans. Once it was heated, cornmeal or flour was dropped into the boiling mixture. When the meal or flour was done, it would rise to the top and float. Some called it cornpone dumplings. Pot liquor dumplings were served to the field slaves, the yard slaves, and the children in the cabins. It was eaten with a spoon, sipped from a bowl, or drunk from a cup.

Pot liquor was at one time a Southern staple. As the mustard greens, turnip greens, collard greens, and meat were cooking, the nutrients seeped into the liquid. When eaten by the slave, the pot liquor strengthened the slave's body. This was by no means deliberate—it just happened—but the value did not go unnoticed. Some of the "black mammies" probably used the cure of pot liquor on their white charges. (My grandmother's theory was that if a child who had chicken pox ate meat, the meat would set the pox marks on the skin. Pot liquor was the answer.)

The strength and endurance the slaves displayed as they toiled under oppression was remarkable. Pot liquor became an important ingredient in their diet. It is said to have been given to the slaves as a healing potion, and they used it to cure chicken pox, measles, and mumps.

A cup of hot mustard-green pot liquor would aid in cooling a high fever. Pot liquor also helped the common cold, and on a chilly day, a cup of pot liquor from greens or meat could warm the very center of one's being.

My grandmother was a firm believer in the power of pot liquor, and so am I. It's like the Jewish mother's faith in chicken soup. And what is chicken soup other than plain old chicken pot liquor?

Sometimes I think about the ingredients that came together to make me who I am today. They weren't big or rare mixtures of complex variety, but simple homegrown compounds. I've not been too unhappy with the product, just confused sometimes about its purpose. Upon close examination of the product—me—I find I developed like the pot liquor. A mixture of heritage and birthrights, difficulties and good fortune, a little of that and mostly whatever, is my combination.

My attempts to explain portions of myself as a small child are placed before you on these pages. You will read that I suffered from a speech impediment in my early years. By the time you meet my family in these pages, you will understand where I got the strength—the pot liquor—to overcome this and eventually become, of all things, a professional storyteller.

Today I live in central North Carolina, a stone's

throw from my grandparents' house at Second Creek, where I spent most of my childhood in the late 1940s and '50s. Although I spend most of my time touring the country, this place travels with me, shaping the stories I tell and giving me the reasons for sharing them.

Some of the ingredients in these pages are anecdotes from my childhood; others are the stories told in my family that have nourished me in good times and bad. They may not be big or monumental, just little things of seemingly small significance; but these stories, tales, and anecdotes were pot liquor to my life.

❧

Grandpa

My grandfather, James Carson, was the son of a slave named Samuel Mitchell Carson. Grandpa was quite proud of the family history, and he never forgot to tell me about it. He talked to me of his father's many exploits and adventures as a slave, and of the trials that his family endured as free men.

The struggle must have been a difficult one, because Pa often looked sad as he remembered the details of his stories. I would look in the same direction that he was looking in, hoping to see what he seemed to see as he talked and stared off in the distance. There was never anything there that was visible to me. I remember water welling up in his eyes as he told some long-lost tale of a journey that was predestined to end in tragedy. Other times the corners of his lips would give him away, turning up into a smile before it was even time for him to deliver the main punch line of the story. He was a very meticulous storyteller.

His thoughts were always ahead of his actual words; he anticipated the actions of the tale, and his face would always give him away.

As I came to know my grandfather as a friend, I realized that he was different from the other men in the family. He never worked, but he gardened and helped in the kitchen, sharpening my grandmother's knives. He spent a lot of time at the house of his sister, my Aunt Sally. He often took long walks.

He rarely went into town. I would sometimes go to Salisbury with whoever was designated to run errands, and whenever I left, I would always say, "What do you want from town, Pa?"

And he would always reply: "Well now, I believe I could use a stack of fifty-dollar bills."

He spent time with me, but there were times when he preferred being alone. These were the times when I couldn't walk with him or be with him in the garden. These were the times when I couldn't understand what was wrong and why he couldn't take me along with him. My grandmother seemed to understand and would not let me bother him.

Why was he like this? I would wonder in confusion. What was wrong with my grandfather when these times occurred? As a child I really never understood, but many years and many stories later—stories from my uncles, aunts, and mother—I was able to put together the story of my grandfather.

Back in the days when my grandparents had only six children—Lawrence, William, Mildred, Ceola, Leonard, and James—they had a prosperous farm, with chickens in the yard, cows, a goat, and a garden that provided vegetables for eating, canning, and preserving. Just behind the house there was an area dug into the ground, six feet deep and six feet wide, and lined with shelves filled with jars of beans, beets, corn, tomatoes, squash, cucumber pickles, watermelon rind pickles, apples, peaches, jams, jellies, and preserves of all description.

Inside the house, the dresser drawers were filled with handmade linens and spreads and quilts of many colors and patterns. The children dressed in good handmade clothes that were warm in the winter and cool in the hot summer.

The family owned a wagon and two good stout mules. My grandfather worked as a yardman in Salisbury for several white people. My grandmother washed and ironed for whites who brought their laundry to her in Carson Town. These jobs did not produce a lot of money, but they allowed the family to enjoy a "fair-to-middling" kind of existence.

One year in May, my grandmother realized that Ceola was not feeling well. My grandmother was known as a healer in the community, and for one week, she used all of her expertise to try to heal her. She used every herb tea, root salve, and medicine that she knew about, to no avail. By the end of the week,

Ceola, who was about twelve years old, was too sick to move, and a doctor was summoned to Carson Town. Everyone in the family was at home when the doctor arrived, except Grandpa, who got home as quickly as he could and arrived shortly before the doctor left. Ceola seemed to be his favorite child, though he tried not to show it.

As he entered the house, the doctor removed quarantine signs from his bag and nailed them to the front door. This meant that everyone in stayed in and everyone out stayed out, until the quarantine was lifted. Ceola had diphtheria.

As the disease progressed, the family turned inward. Groceries had to be obtained by sending a note, pinned to a mule named Dexter, to Aunt Sally. She would then place the flour, sugar, canned milk, coffee, and other necessities on the mule's back and point him home. The doctor visited once every two weeks. First he would examine Ceola, and then the other members of the family. No one else was ever infected by the disease, but the doctor left the quarantine signs up because Ceola was still quite ill.

After each visit, the doctor demanded payment. The small amount of money in savings was quickly gone. Soon my grandparents were paying the doctor with eggs and butter, then whole chickens, goat's milk, fresh garden produce, and canned produce. After a while, the family had no stores of food left, not in the root cellar under the house, not in the milk pit.

The garden was empty, and there were very few people in the community who could afford to help.

My Aunt Mildred, who tells that she was thirteen years old at the time, remembers watching her brothers set traps for birds. My grandmother would sometimes cry when five or six birds were all they had to cook. Although wintertime was hard, they were able to hunt rabbit, raccoon, and possum in order to put meat on the table. When spring arrived at last, Ceola's health began to improve. She was able to eat and sit up longer. She read her Bible to my grandpa, to his delight, and sometimes she would even sing for him. He was so happy when she began to improve, and he visited her bedside frequently.

Signs of spring were evident throughout the countryside. My grandmother made several trips to the woods to gather young herbs for teas, roots for poultices, and pine and cedar for the air in the house.

One day, Pa had just finished burning the dried weed from the place he would plow for his garden when he came in to get a hot cup of tea to drink. When Grandma told him Ceola had asked for him, he drank the tea and went directly to her bed. She told him she had learned a new passage in the Bible and read it to him.

Then she sang for him. I've heard that her choice of songs was "Jacob's Ladder," but some say it was "Swing Low, Sweet Chariot." Whatever it was, she sang it then as sweetly as any angel. That day, she was well again and everyone was happy. Grandma cautioned Pa not to tire her out, and he agreed. He took her Bible, placed it on the table beside her bed, kissed her forehead, and tucked the covers around her neck. She smiled and closed her eyes to sleep.

Over in the night, my Grandmother stopped to check Ceola, and found, sadly, that she had died.

My grandpa never quite got over that.

I believe he suffered depression from then on. The pain of losing a child, coupled with losing all that they had accumulated, caused him so much confusion that he became mentally ill for a long period of time. The mental illness must have soon developed into physical pain, and by the time I came onto the scene, the suffering had taken its toll.

My grandpa thought I was the cutest, smartest, sweetest child that had ever lived. At least, that's the impression I got. I remember being given a recitation for a Sunday school Christmas program. I must have been about four years old. It was a simple speech: "Today is Christmas Day, Merry Christmas to you!"

My grandma and grandpa helped me learn it and say it just right. We'd sit down to supper and after the prayer, as Grandma tied my napkin around my neck, Grandpa would ask me to say my speech and I would speak right up. "Today is Christmas Day, Merry Christmas to you!" My grandpa would grin and say with a giggle, "That girl's gonna be president!" My grandma would grunt and shrug her shoulders.

Then the day for the recitation came. When I stood in the front of the church, the grown-ups were listening intently and admiring all the children in their new clothes. I stood in front of that congregation scared to death! My grandparents sat smiling and admiring their wonderful grandchild and my Aunt Sally, who was in charge of the program, said, "Speak up, go on now … talk."

I started to say, "Today is Christmas Day…." But then someone sneezed, distracting me, and I forgot my speech and said: "Happy Easter!"

Grandpa turned to Grandma and said, "Are you sure that gal's got good sense?"

And he was the one who said I'd be president!

Even though I may have disappointed him, he still invited me to accompany him on his long walks. In the summer, we would check on his garden. Sometimes we'd work in the garden. He would pull weeds and I'd pull vegetable plants. He would always stop me before too much damage was done.

Grandpa walked with a cane. When I was quite small, he would put the cane to rest as he was sitting and I would pick it up and run away with it. I own that cane now. I guess it was merely a prop for him because it was just a piece of lightweight bamboo. It couldn't have supported him very much or been much help in walking. I remember him using it as a pointer, to give directions to people. He even used it to knock on doors.

Sometimes we'd walk up the path to my great-aunt Sally's house. He would tire by the time we mounted the short hill and would sit down on the floor of the back porch, turn, and use the cane to knock on the floor of the porch, calling Aunt Sally at the same time.

I liked Aunt Sally a lot. She was a large woman, with shiny black hair that she kept in a ball at the nape of her neck. When she smiled, she showed a glimmer of gold on her front teeth. She always smelled sweet to me, like a freshly baked cake. I found out later that she used vanilla flavoring as a perfume.

Aunt Sally was multi-talented—a cook, a quilter, a singer, and a piano player. I also remember her as a practical joker. Most of the jokes were directed toward my grandma, who was afraid of her own shadow at times.

On the hottest day of one summer—I would have been three or four—Pa had gone to town with one of my uncles. Grandma and I were left at home. I was playing on the porch, and my grandma was sweeping the yard. (Grass never stood a chance with Grandma. She hated chicken droppings in the yard, so she'd often sweep three or four times a day.)

All of a sudden we heard Aunt Sally's call: "Whooo—whoa, Ola!"

My grandma stopped sweeping and looked up

toward the hill at Aunt Sally's house and answered her call, "Whoo, Sally! Whatcha want?"

"Oh Lord, Ola, ain't you heard? They say a convict's done got loose from the chain gang. He might be headed this way," yelled Aunt Sally.

"Oh Lord, Sally, what we gonna do?" said my grandma, fear welling up in her voice.

"Lock your doors, Ola, lock your doors!" The way her voice trailed off, we knew she was locking up, too.

My grandma went to work. She dragged me in from the porch, closed all the windows and locked all the doors, and pulled down every shade in the house. We sat in the far corner of the bedroom in the dark for what seemed like hours. With every noise we heard, I could hear her whispering a prayer. "Oh, Lord Jesus, help us, help us, Father, help us." Eventually the combination of darkness and heat caused me to fall asleep.

I was finally awakened by my grandpa's voice at the front door. "Ola, unlock the door! What in the name of God is wrong?"

Grandma rushed to the door to open it, and when she did, the feel of fresh, cool air swept over me. I felt rather sick. It must have had the same effect on Grandma because Uncle Will rushed in and caught her before she fell and helped her to the porch. She was soaking wet with sweat.

As Uncle Will ran in the house and got her

smelling salts, Grandpa stood there looking at both of us, shaking his head from side to side. "Ola," he said, "what was you doin' all locked up in the house as blame hot as it is?"

"Lord, Jim, right after you left, Sally told me there was a convict on the loose from the chain gang out here and I thought we'd better lock up."

"Jesus Christ, Ola, that convict was way on the other side of Lexington, sixteen miles away. I wish you'd quit listening to Sally; you know she's full of fool and folly all the time."

That was just one of many times that Aunt Sally had a good laugh off my grandma. It bothered Pa when Aunt Sally played such tricks, but he never got too upset. Sometimes he even laughed.

When we walked together he walked very slowly, so I never had any trouble keeping up. He'd point out things of interest and importance, things he thought I should know. "You see this chimney? I put every one of these bricks here myself. Made 'em with my own two hands. Bum'bees nest in here so you be careful not to get too close." His voice dropped to a whisper: "You may get stung." Now the thing that was going through my mind was, *What's a bum'bee?*

We'd walk past Aunt Sally's and up the road. There was a slight hill, which would slow him down even more. I'd hear a grunt now and then, but he never complained. Once, as he stopped to rest, he took his cane and dug around in the dried leaves in the ditch. He found something and lifted it from the ground on the edge of his cane so that I could see it.

"Hey," he said loudly, "look what I found."

Well, hanging there on the end of his cane was a wiggling, squirming, long black snake.

"Grandpa, look! Look, Grandpa, look, it's a snake!" I yelled. "Throw it down, throw it down!"

"Oh, he's not gonna hurt you. This is a king snake," replied Grandpa. "They don't like to bite people. They like rats and things that get into the barn and eat the corn and grain. We try not to kill them. We'd rather just throw them back so they can help us some more."

As he turned and threw it into the woods, Pa's explanation didn't help me much. I was still shaking from being so close to that snake. He put his hand on my back and patted me rather hard and said as he chuckled and squeezed me toward his leg, "Don't worry my girl, that ol' snake would rather suck on you than bite you."

I remember those walks because we were always exploring. Sometimes when the conversation seemed at a loss, I took over. I liked to ask questions.

"What's that, Pa?"

"That's a pine tree," he'd explain.

"And that right there, what's that?"

"That's a rock," he'd say.

But those questions, I think, sometimes got on his nerves, and I could always tell when he was tired of answering because the answers turned into grunts and groans—"un huh, uh huh"—and then he'd yawn and say, "Wait, hush, did you hear something?"

Well, of course I heard nothing, but I stopped to listen just the same. As we stood perfectly still in the middle of the road, out of the woods, running just as fast as he could, was a little brown rabbit. Startled by it, I moved closer to Pa. But he assured me there was nothing that would hurt me.

"What was that, Pa?" I'd say.

"It was ol' Br'er Rabbit himself."

I knew that, but you could not get a story by being too smart.

Our walk would usually turn back to Aunt Sally's porch or to the apple tree in her front yard where the stump of another tree made a good seat for Pa. He would then tell me of some special adventure of Br'er Rabbit or some of Br'er Rabbit's associates who were frequent visitors to the Big Road.

Some of Pa's tales I easily remember. I never know what may trigger them in my memory: the cool shade of a tree like my Aunt Sally's apple tree, or the scent of coffee brewing, bread baking, or some long-lost texture of fabric that reminds me of my baby quilt or a coat or dress I once wore that Grandma made.

The tales that he recounted to me about his father's slave days were sometimes puzzling. I could hear a tightening in his throat as he told of his father's problems and triumphs as a slave in Rowan County. If we were at Aunt Sally's house, she would help him tell about ol' Massa and the slave named Mitchell, who never knew how old he was, who never knew his mother or father, and who had no last name until his master asked if he wanted one. His master gave him his first and last names: Samuel Mitchell Carson.

Mitchell was the one who slept at the master's feet because of his master's painful struggle with gout. He was unable to move about easily, so Mitchell helped him in and out of bed, on and off wagons, and onto his horse.

Since the master's wife was unable to read or write, the master was the only one able to conduct business. Not being a well man, this was sometimes difficult. So during these times, in the privacy of the "big house," the master taught Samuel Mitchell Carson how to read and write—against the law, mind you! Without anyone knowing, the slave signed papers and conducted a lot of the master's business.

My great-grandfather was freed in 1869 and given fifty acres of land, where he started his family, began a school for children in that settlement, and became the preacher of what became known as Carson Town.

As I listened to the tales of my great-grandfather,

the pride Pa had for his family was passed on to me. It grew and grew, and has helped mold me. No matter what happens to me now, I remember that I came from proud people, people who made a difference in the world a long time ago. My ancestors would not be pleased if I were satisfied with not being all that I can be.

One night, when I was close to five, I heard a lot of noise and movement downstairs. I slipped quietly down the stairs and saw Grandma, Aunt Mildred, and my mother rushing in and out of Grandpa's room with sheets, blankets, and wash pans of water. I could hear him coughing as I crept closer. As I peered in his room, I saw blood on the bed sheets and on the floor beside his bed. My mother and Aunt Mildred were wiping his face and cleaning up around him, rushing from place to place. My grandma was holding him, her arms wrapped around his shoulders. I didn't know exactly what was going on, but I watched until I fell asleep on the stairs.

The next day, my mother dressed me and told me that we were going to town for a few days. I went in to tell Grandpa goodbye and that I'd be back soon.

"What do you want from town, Pa?"

I waited for him to ask for his stack of fifty-dollar bills. But he didn't say anything this time.

Just as I turned to remind him of his usual

response, I noticed a faint smile cross his face. He waved his hand slowly.

I didn't think this was the time to say anymore. When I returned three or four days later, my Pa was no longer in bed.

"Where's Pa?" I asked.

My grandma said, "He's gone to heaven. And no," she said quietly before I could ask, "when you go to heaven you don't come back."

I never saw my grandpa again. I wasn't so sure if I liked this place called heaven.

A Ghost Story:
Pa's Trip from Town

One Sunday afternoon all the folks were gathered on Aunt Sally's front porch. Uncle Fred had just picked his guitar and sung one of his favorite songs. Everybody had enjoyed a bowl of homemade ice cream and a slice of Aunt Sally's pound cake.

Somebody asked Grandpa, "Jim, do you remember that time you came in from town and stopped at the Hall house? What really happened to you that night?"

That was all the asking he needed. My grandpa smiled and hesitated for a moment as he shifted his weight on his chair, moving slowly as if trying to recall the incident. Some overly anxious person spoke up and asked him again if he remembered.

"'Course I remembers," he said, "I remembers it as if it happened the day before yesterday. Ola needed black thread, vanilla flavoring, and a bottle of Hadacol. Will was

out here that morning, and he drove me to town. I didn't want to wait all day for him, so I got what I come for and got on the road back to Second Creek. It must have been around two-thirty or three when I noticed the sky begin to get dark with storm clouds. I was beginning to worry 'cause Ola never liked storms and I knew there was nobody home with her but that little young'un and she couldn't be of no help to a person scared of thunder and lightning."

Pa shifted his cane from one hand to the other. We took this as our cue to sit back and get comfortable. We were in for a story.

I quickened my steps, but the rain was quicker than me and it was coming down hard. Never seen such hard rain. One or two drops hit me on my back and nearly knocked me to the ground. I knew I couldn't stand much of that, so I looked up to see exactly where I was and I knew right off I was at the Hall house.

I went fast as I could to the porch. When I stepped up on the porch, the bottom fell out of the sky. You couldn't see your hand before your face. I would have stayed on the porch, but the lightning was getting bad and the rain was that blowing kind of rain. I'd have been soaked to the bone if I had stood there any longer. I turned to see if I could get into the house, and lo and behold, the front door was open. I knew when I first stepped up on that porch that the door wasn't open. If I had had good sense I would have turned around right then and there and took my chances in the storm. Instead, I went on in the house and found myself in the strangest place I have ever seen in my life. I had always heard tell that that old house was different, but nobody could've prepared me for what I saw.

The house had been empty for years and years, but there wasn't a sign of dust or dirt or wear and tear on the inside. The furniture sat about like someone had just placed it there. Pictures on the wall were bright and colorful. Every time lightning would strike, I could see more and more. I walked into another room and as the lightning struck, I looked up the stairway. There, standing in a line, was seven young girls all dressed in evening dresses ... all smiling and laughing like there was a party or a dance going on. I got to feeling kind of scared, so I stepped back behind a curtain at a glass door and peeked through it. As each girl reached the bottom of the steps, she waltzed out onto the floor as if someone had taken her hand. As they all danced and circled the floor, I felt like I was watching something that took place every day and night.

They say the man and woman who lived in this house, the Halls, had seven daughters. They were all beautiful beyond belief. Old man Hall was pretty well off, so he wanted his daughters to marry well. Young men by the dozens courted and begged for the hand of each young woman, but Daddy and Mama Hall never thought anyone was good enough for their daughters. They had parties every night—picnics, dances, all kinds of parties to entice the right young men as suitors, but nobody ever came close to pleasing them.

The youngest of the seven sisters fell ill with scarlet fever and died. After her death, one by one, the other sisters fell ill and passed on, until there was no one left but the father. Some folks say he died of a broken heart. There were no relatives that anybody knew of, so the house was deserted and nobody had touched it for years.

I kept watching this ghostly dance until I realized the rain had stopped. The storm was over and the sky began to lighten up again. As it lightened, I could see the inside of the house much better. What I had mistaken for furniture in good shape was old and broken; dust and dirt clung to the walls, which had holes and big water spots. The dancers had started back up the stairway. What I had taken for beautiful young women were skeletons with hunks of hair clinging to their naked skulls, and rags of torn and dirty dresses clinging to dry bones that clicked and clacked as they clamored up the steps. After realizing what I had just seen, I backed out of the door and down the steps as fast as I could go. When I got to the road and looked back toward the house, I saw the figure of a man standing in the door shaking his fist at me and then

the door slammed ...
Bam!

Bam! Pa had just thrown his cane on the floor and frightened everyone within earshot.

"My God, Mr. Jim," said one of his listeners, "is that the truth?"

"Well, son," said Pa, "it's as true as I can ever tell." I watched as he moved the clump of tobacco from one side of his jaw to the other. When he made that kind of move I knew that that tobacco hid the smile that crossed his face.

Br'er Rabbit
Builds a Home

My Grandpa and I were walkers. We walked to his garden every day. We walked up the hill to see his brother, Uncle Fred. We walked to his sister Aunt Sally's house and down the road to see Aunt Mag, his sister in-law.

Pa would sometimes wait until Grandma had me busy somewhere else or I was down for a nap before he would leave. I never understood that maybe he didn't want my company all the time. But when I discovered he had left without me, there was just no living with me until he returned.

Early morning walks were the best. The road was shaded by the trees. The sun was not yet beaming down on us, and the day was quiet and still. The birds and other animals in the woods were still running about—deer, chipmunks, foxes, raccoons, possums, rats, squirrels, rabbits—especially rabbits. They were always with us on the road.

When we'd spot one running ahead of us or behind us or right beside us, Pa would say Br'er Rabbit was going about his daily business.

I remember asking Pa if Br'er Rabbit had a house to live in like me and him. In reply, he related the story of how Br'er Rabbit built a home.

All the creatures in the Big Wood—Br'er Possum, Br'er Bear, Br'er Coon, Br'er Wolf, and Br'er Rabbit—decided they should go in together and build themselves a house.

They each took different jobs. Br'er Rabbit insisted that he'd have to do something on the ground because he couldn't climb ladders, which made him dizzy in the head. And he couldn't work outside because the sun made him shiver. So he got himself a ruler and stuck a pencil behind his ear and started measuring and marking, marking and measuring. He was in and out, all around, so busy that the other creatures really thought he was putting down a whole passel of work. Yet all the while, he was just marking time, doing absolutely nothing.

The critters that was workin', was workin'. They built a fine house, the likes of which nobody in those parts had ever seen. Why, if the truth be known, it was a splendid house: plenty of upstairs rooms, plenty of downstairs rooms, a whole heap of chimneys, fireplaces, and all sorts of other wonderful things.

After the house was finished, each critter picked a room. Old Br'er Rabbit picked one of the upstairs rooms and proceeded to furnish it. While all the other critters were busy finishing their rooms, Br'er Rabbit was slipping three things into his room: a shotgun, a big black cannon, and a big tin tub of water.

When everything was all finished in the house, they cooked a big supper to celebrate. Then everyone took a seat in the parlor.

Br'er Rabbit sat for awhile, and then he yawned and stretched and excused himself for bed. The other creatures stayed on and laughed and talked and had a good time in their new parlor.

While they were talking and laughing, Br'er Rabbit yelled from his room, "When a big feller like me wants to sit down, whereabouts do you think he ought to sit?"

All the other critters just laughed and said, "When a big feller like you can't sit in a chair, he better sit on the floor."

"Watch out down there, 'cause I'm fixing to sit right now," yelled Br'er Rabbit. He pulled the trigger of the shotgun. *Ka-boom!*

Well, all the critters looked at one another and wondered, what in the world was that? But everything was quiet then, and nobody said anything for a long time.

After a while, the critters forgot the noise and

started talking and laughing again.

Then Br'er Rabbit stuck his head out the door again and said, "When a big feller like me wants to sneeze, whereabouts can he sneeze?"

The other creatures turned and hollered up the stairs, "When a big feller like you can't hold a sneeze, he can sneeze where he pleases."

"Watch out down there cause I'm gonna sneeze right here," said Br'er Rabbit. And he lit the fuse on the cannon. *Ka-boom!*

Well, the sound of the cannon knocked the critters out of their chairs. The glass shook in the windows, the dishes rattled in the cupboard, and Br'er Bear hit the floor, right on his bottom.

"Lordsey be," said Br'er Bear, "I think Br'er Rabbit has a powerful bad cold. I think I'm gonna step outside for a breath of fresh air."

All the critters settled down again and were talking among themselves, when Br'er Rabbit yelled out another time. "When a big feller like me wants to take a chew of tobacco, whereabouts is he supposed to spit?"

The other critters hollered back to Br'er Rabbit, mad as they could be, "If you be a big man or a little man, spit where you please."

"Look out down there!" yelled Br'er Rabbit, "I'm gonna spit!" About that time he turned over the tub of water and it came rolling down the steps. *Ker-splash!*

Well, every one of the critters heard it coming at

the same time. They all took off in different directions. Some jumped out of the windows, some bolted through the doors, everyone went in a different direction, but they all cleared out of the house.

Old Br'er Rabbit locked the doors, closed the windows, went to bed, and slept like he owned the world.

Br'er Rabbit Gets Caught

Uncle James and Pa often told this story. Now I know about four different versions of this story. Everyone who tells it tells it differently.

This version is a bit of Uncle James, a bit of Pa, and a bit of Mrs. Corrine Thomas, the librarian of Monroe Street School—my elementary school librarian.

Br'er Rabbit had been running that day till he couldn't run any longer. Br'er Wolf was after him.

He was so close on Br'er Rabbit that all that rabbit could do was hide in a hollow tree to think and rest. The hole was too little for Br'er Wolf, so he just lay down outside the hollow tree to think and rest.

While Br'er Wolf was lying there, Br'er Turkey Buzzard came flapping by and lit on a branch of the hollow tree.

Br'er Turkey Buzzard looked at Br'er Wolf and

said to himself, "Looks like Br'er Wolf is dead. I'm real sorry about that."

"No, I ain't dead," said Br'er Wolf. "I got ol' Br'er Rabbit pent up in this here tree. I'm gonna get him this time if it takes me till New Year's Eve."

"How you gonna get him out?" asked Br'er Turkey Buzzard.

"I'm gonna cut him out," said Br'er Wolf. "If you stay here and watch the hole while I go home to get my ax, I'll give you a choice piece of him before I cook him."

So Br'er Wolf loped off down the road and Br'er Turkey Buzzard took up his watch outside the hole.

By and by Br'er Rabbit hollered out of the hole, "Br'er Wolf! Br'er Wolf! Oh, Br'er Wolf!"

Br'er Wolf was gone, and Br'er Turkey Buzzard kept quiet.

"Br'er Wolf," yelled Br'er Rabbit, "you don't have to say nothing. I know you're out there. I just wanted to tell you that I sure wish Br'er Turkey Buzzard was here."

Then Br'er Turkey Buzzard got curious. He wanted to know why, so he changed his voice to sound like Br'er Wolf. "What you want with Br'er Turkey Buzzard?"

"Oh nothing much. 'Cept this hole has a bunch of fat gray squirrels that Br'er Turkey Buzzard would find mighty tasty," said Br'er Rabbit.

"How he gonna get 'em?" said Br'er Turkey

Buzzard.

"It's just a little hole round the other side of this tree. If Br'er Turkey Buzzard was here, he could stand outside and I could drive 'em out to him," said Br'er Rabbit.

"Drive 'em out then," said Br'er Turkey Buzzard. "I'll see that Br'er Turkey Buzzard gets 'em."

Then Br'er Rabbit kicked up a powerful noise like he was driving something out. Br'er Turkey Buzzard happened round to the other side to catch the squirrels when they ran out.

Br'er Rabbit lit out fast, and down the road he ran.

Br'er Rabbit and the Little Brown Jug

My granddaddy and I had a love for hot biscuits with butter and molasses. We also ate fatback meat with our biscuits. I do believe this story was told during one of these favorite meals.

Br'er Rabbit always cautioned his children about the dangers of the world. He told them to always be on their feet, keep their eyes open, and keep their ears up and listening.

One day Br'er Rabbit had to go off on business. He left all his children playing in the yard. By and by, along came Br'er Fox and Br'er Wolf.

Br'er Wolf said to Br'er Fox, "Look at them little fat rabs. All I'd have to do is snatch out their ears, cut off their tails, and skin 'em and eat 'em."

Br'er Fox said, "Shut your mouth! That sounds *so* good. Come on, let's get us one."

Br'er Wolf said, "If we wait we can get all of 'em. Just make sure Br'er Rabbit ain't nowhere around. But if he comes along somebody needs to keep him busy while somebody else grabs the rabs. I'll grab the rabs while you keep Br'er Rabbit busy."

"No, no, no!" yelled Br'er Wolf. "The rabs will all be eat up when I get there. You keep Br'er Rabbit busy while *I* catch the rabs, then I'll give you half the ones I catch."

The fight between Br'er Wolf and Br'er Fox started. Teeth and fur flew every which away.

The little rabbits got scared and started running down the road. They were running so fast they didn't realize that Br'er Rabbit was right in front of them.

"Daddy, Daddy, Daddy," cried the little rabbits.

"Wait, wait a minute," said Br'er Rabbit. "What are you children doing away from home?" As he said that, Br'er Rabbit leaned over and slipped a brown jug from his shoulder.

"What's in the jug, Daddy, what's in the jug?"

"Well," said Br'er Rabbit, "I can show you better than I can tell you." Br'er Rabbit removed the cork from the jug and let each little rabbit lick the cork.

"What was that, Daddy, what was that?" asked the little rabbits.

"Well, young'uns, that's what we call mo-lasses."

"Give us molasses, daddy, molasses!" they

yelled.

"'Course I will, but first we'll go home and bake us some cat-head biscuits. Then we get some sweet butter and pour the molasses over the butter and mix the butter and the molasses real good. Then we'll lay that cat-head biscuit on that molasses and butter and we'll sop and eat, sop and eat, sop and eat."

When Br'er Rabbit said *eat*, the little rabbits remembered just why they were running. "Daddy, Daddy, Br'er Wolf and Br'er Fox say they're gonna skin us and eat us."

"Don't you worry," said Br'er Rabbit. "We'll see just who Br'er Fox and Br'er Wolf are gonna skin and eat." Br'er Rabbit picked up his jug and started home. He hid the little rabbits in the woods before he left.

As he walked up on Br'er Wolf and Br'er Fox, they stopped fighting. They all spoke, and Br'er Rabbit asked what they were doing. Br'er Wolf said they were speculating. Br'er Fox said he would like to continue to speculate but he needed to head on down the road. Br'er Fox winked at Br'er Wolf, and Br'er Wolf winked back. Br'er Fox went on his way while Br'er Wolf and Br'er Rabbit passed the time of day.

Br'er Wolf said, "And what's that you've got there in your jug?"

"Why don't you taste it, and maybe you'll know what it is."

Br'er Wolf licked the cork. "Whoo my!" yelled Br'er Wolf. "That's sure 'nough good. What is it?"

Br'er Rabbit said, "Well, I'll tell you, Br'er Wolf. I'm scared to tell you what it is."

"Don't you worry yourself," said Br'er Wolf. "Just tell me."

Br'er Rabbit seem nervous. "Well, it's like this. It's fox blood!"

"It what?" exclaimed Br'er Wolf. "Fox blood! Are you sure?"

"I knows what I knows."

"You mean this is …?"

"That's what I mean," said Br'er Rabbit, "that's what I mean."

"How do you get it?" said Br'er Wolf, "How do you get it?"

"Everybody gets it for themselves. You get yours, and I get mine. But I will tell you that the fresher it is, the better it is."

Br'er Wolf excused himself and went on down the road.

After a while, Br'er Rabbit heard Br'er Fox pleading and begging for his life. "Please, Br'er Wolf, why you have that big old club in your hand? You weren't gonna hit me, were you?"

Br'er Rabbit threw his head back and laughed good and hard. "I fooled them again," he said. "I fooled them again."

Grandma

My grandma's name was Ola Hannah Carson. It was my grandma who showed me the importance of pot liquor. Pot liquor was the liquid from mustard greens, collard greens, peas, pinto beans, white potatoes, beef, chicken—anything stewed or boiled, anything that was a liquid broth—it was all considered pot liquor.

There were special pot liquors for special seasons. In the spring, dried sulfur was mixed with the pot liquors of boiled poke salad as a "cleaning out" tonic. In the winter, yellow onions were boiled, and the pot liquor from that was mixed with honey and whiskey. That was a powerful cough syrup!

Sometimes I would inquire as to what my grandma was drinking in her cup. She'd say, "I'm drinking a 'lie-lower-to-catch-a-meddler.'" It really was a cup of pot liquor made from mustard and turnip greens. That was her favorite. She'd drink the pot liquor before she'd eat the greens. The greens were, of course, seasoned with fatback or ham hock or some sort of seasoning meat, so the pot liquor always had a nice taste.

My grandma used pot liquor to cure all sorts of things, from an earache to an ingrown toenail. I think my grandma had a cure for everything—and lots of other folks thought so, too. They came to see her for medicine. She knew all kinds of cures from roots and plants in the woods, from the bark of trees in the front yard, and even from different parts of the innards of cows and pigs and chickens and sheep, of all things.

Her wood stove never got cold. She would boil on the stove, bake in the ashes of the fireplace, and fry fish in an open pot outside. Pa used to make a fire under her big black pot in the yard so that she could make soap, apple butter, and other things. She boiled water to dip chickens into so that the feathers would come off easily. She boiled muslin to bleach it white. She boiled onion skins, green grass, walnut hulls, poke berries, and red mud to make a dye for clothes and yards of new material for sewing.

The spring and summer were the most interesting times with Grandma. In early spring, we went into the woods to gather. We picked young fern plants. She would dig up their little curled heads as they came up through the dead leaves. The ground was usually wet, so she could dig easily. Bark, flowers, the roots from cattails—she'd dry them all, and if you had a stomachache, she'd give you a little tiny piece of cattail to chew.

The summer when I was four years old, I remember that I had real playmates. I had always been the only child in the house with my grandparents, except those times my cousins came to play. These new playmates were the children of some of the hands who worked the white farm above our home. I had first seen them one day when I was on the side porch. Three white children came down through the pasture and crawled under the barbed-wire fence, yelling and laughing like somebody was after them. When they stopped to rest, they discovered me on the porch watching them. They were just as surprised as I was.

The three boys looked to be about eight, five, and three. They came over to the porch and spoke to me. They wanted to know if I lived there and what my name was. I answered their questions.

They immediately took a liking to my toys, especially my mechanical ferris wheel that had a red clown face in the middle of the spokes. They wound it and wound it and made it go so fast that it caused the littlest one with them to squeal with delight. My grandma, knowing that was not my squeal, looked out the back door. I will never forget how she said, "Good Lord, have mercy, where in the world did you three come from?"

They stood there looking at my grandma with pitiful grins on their faces. Looking at them through Grandma's eyes, I could now see that their teeth were rotten and their clothes were dirty and ragged. They were barefoot and the lower part of their legs were filled with wet, running sores.

The smallest child was the only one who didn't seem to be scared. He started talking, but nobody could understand one word. From his pocket he handed Grandma some broken marbles and some caps from Coca-Cola bottles. I guess he was offering gifts to her. She thanked him and said that she wouldn't take his playthings.

Finally the oldest boy told us that they had been playing in the pasture, not knowing there was a bull about. That was what caused them to plunge through the barbed wire.

"Well, you children have to go home. Your mama's worried about you," said my grandma.

They tried to convince my grandma that their mother really didn't care where they were, but she stood firm. From that day on, those little boys would show up at some point every day. They knew I liked their broken marbles, rocks, and bottle caps, so they brought me lots of them in return for time with my toys—as much time as they could squeeze in before my grandma ran them off.

One day their mother appeared. She was over-weight and a little dirty herself. She had two little dirty-faced babies, one in each arm, and three more children in addition to my playmates. They were all filled with sores, even the mother.

She started off by telling Grandma that I was the "cutest little pickaninny" she had ever seen. You could see that my grandma was upset when she heard that, but she was polite to the woman and asked her what she needed.

She said Mr. Huffman had told her that Grandma could help her get rid of the sores on their legs. My grandma agreed and started inside, but she must have thought better of leaving me there because she came back on the porch and took me by the hand and nearly dragged me inside with her.

When we returned to the porch, Grandma painted them all with some sort of purple salve. As they headed toward the path with purple arms and legs, backs and necks, I could hear Grandma muttering, "Pestilence, just pure pestilence. Fleas, mosquitoes, flies, ticks, pestilence. My Lord from Zion!" She continued to talk to herself as she washed her hands in the dishpan outside. We never saw them again.

Grandma was quite protective of me. But I was later told it had not always been that way. Once upon a time, my relatives said, my grandmother disliked me. You see, I was the daughter of her youngest girl, Mae Troy. My mother and father never married, and out of

Grandma's thirteen children, there had never been an illegitimate birth in the family. She was sure that my mother had brought disgrace to the family. But she must have overcome some of those feelings, because I don't remember any distance between us. I always remember a kind and loving but stern woman who took care of me all the time.

As I was just a little tot, there wasn't very much in the way of helping that I could do. That's why I spent a lot of time with Pa. He was not able to help her because of his sickness, so he kept me company while my grandma ran the house.

Grandma and I looked after each other. She showed me the place where she kept her smelling salts and camphor. I was to go after them if she looked faint or sick. I still have the little tin cup where she kept her medicine.

She in turn protected me from people who laughed at me because of my speech problem. Because of my impacted teeth, I couldn't move my tongue properly, and so many of my letter sounds were inverted. My family could understand me, but many outside the family could not.

My grandmother saw to it that my every need was met.

My grandmother was a wonderful teller of tales, but my memory of late gets a great jolt when I think about the tales that my mother told me about her own growing-up years. One of the stories that I remember and love very much is the story of the strawberry pie. My mother must have been about nine years old when this happened. She was the youngest girl in the family, but she had a brother, Leroy, who was one year younger. Because the others were much older, she and her baby brother were the best of friends and shared everything, good and bad.

My grandmother kept her baked goods—bread, cake, pies, cookies—in a cabinet called a pie safe. The top shelves were off-limits to the children unless they were told to retrieve something from them. The very bottom shelf was the place where they could obtain a snack—if they asked first. Sugar cakes, sugar biscuits, and cookies could always be found there, and my mother and her brother made frequent trips to the pie safe.

My mother tells of visiting the pie safe one day and finding only cold biscuits. They were good, but Mom and Leroy were searching for sweet things. The top shelves, she knew, always contained pies and cakes for special meals. She decided to find out what was on the top shelf.

The shelf was just an inch or two out of her reach, so she stood on her toes and let her fingers do the searching. As her fingers moved about they moved into a pan with something soft and gooey. She removed her hand and licked her fingers. Strawberry pie! Strawberries were rare because their growing season was short and they just didn't can well, unless they were made into jam or jelly. Fresh strawberry pie was indeed a treat!

When my mother tells this story she always says that her taste buds outweighed her good sense, because first she ate as much as she could hold and then she fed Leroy the rest.

It seems that the pie had been made for the visit of the local preacher on Sunday, which was the next day. The time came to serve the pie, and my grandmother discovered the empty pan. She apologized for not having the promised pie and instead served something else.

After dinner, when the preacher had left, my grandmother asked who ate the pie. No one would admit to having eaten it.

My grandmother said there was only one way to find out who did it. She reached up above the mantelpiece and took down an old double-barreled shotgun. The gun was not in good shape; in fact, it was held together at the barrel and handle with an old, oily rag wrapped around it. She placed the handle of the gun on the floor with the barrel between her knees.

She asked each child to blow into the barrel of the gun. "The gun will smell strawberries on the breath of the guilty one, and it will shoot and blow your head off," she said.

All the children were afraid, but the guilty ones

made their confession, and several other confessions that were not even asked for.

My grandfather then asked if Grandmother intended to punish them.

"No," my grandmother said, "they have already punished themselves."

When Pa died, Aunt Mildred got upset because Grandma was staying way out in the country. Her words were, "They had a time getting Papa's body out of here. I'll never let anybody else go through what I did with Papa." So she and her brothers and sisters moved Grandma and me to town, to Salisbury. We shared a house with my Uncle Nesbert and his wife, Talmadge. They tried to make it like home for her, but it just didn't work. She was frightened by a lot of things. She missed her friends, her home, her everyday surroundings.

When I was about five years old, Grandma and I moved in with Aunt Mildred. About three years later, we all began to notice a great change in Grandma. She was forgetful, not over long periods of time but from moment to moment. Recognizing us caused her some difficulty. She would ask who we were, over and over again.

We discovered that she was hoarding food. She carried her purse with her wherever she went in the house. There was usually nothing in it but a handkerchief and her snuff box, although sometimes she would slip the bread from her plate into her purse.

She talked back to the faces of people on television, answering them as if they had spoken directly to her. Art Linkletter was the one who Grandma had the biggest discussions with, and at the end of the show, when he waved goodbye to the television audience, she would wave and whisper, "Lord, I wish he would just go on. He's said goodbye four times now." Then she would laugh.

We watched her forget simple things like washing the dishes and attending to her own hygiene. Before, she would write long letters to Aunt Malivia in Chicago, and to Aunt Edna and Uncle Leroy. Now she started letters and rarely finished them. When she did, she would write that Aunt Mildred never fed her, never gave her money, and hid her clothes from her. This, of course, hurt Aunt Mildred deeply because she was doing everything humanly possible to make Grandma happy and comfortable.

Uncle Nesbert still dropped her off at the Presbyterian Church every Sunday. One Monday afternoon, Reverend Johnson stopped by the house to see Aunt Mildred. He told her that Grandma should have someone with her at church. The ushers were saying that as the offering plates were passed she would tear paper from the bulletin and drop it into the plate instead of money. All this made me sad and sometimes a little angry. My friend and protector was not herself. What was wrong?

Aunt Mildred took her to Dr. Shoates, our family doctor of many years. He said she was in good health, but her memory loss was due to age and a condition known as hardening of the arteries.

Because of Aunt Mildred's working hours, Grandma was left to take care of herself and me most of the time. One day I waited on pins and needles for my aunt to come home from her morning job. Grandma was planning to leave the house. She said she was going to visit Mrs. Talton, a white lady that Grandma used to wash and iron for. Over the years they had become good friends.

I was scared. I knew Grandma didn't know where she was going, but when I protested, she told me that I was the child and she was the adult; I was to tend to my business and leave hers alone. I didn't know what my next move was to be.

I checked the clock—it was half past eleven, and the West End bus that Aunt Mildred rode always arrived at twelve noon, sharp. I was hoping I could stall Grandma for thirty more minutes until Aunt Mildred got home, but how? She was dressed and ready to leave.

She could not find her handkerchief. I knew where they were kept, so while she was distracted I raced to the dresser drawer, took them out, and hid them under the pillow on the bed. She searched and searched, then finally seemed to forget what it was she had been looking for, and headed toward the door. It was 11:45—just a few more minutes and I'd have it made. Grandma walked toward the door. When she opened it, I yelled, "But you need to fix me something to eat, Grandma. I'm hungry!"

Aunt Mildred always made us lunch when she came home, and Grandma seemed to sense that I was trying to hold her up. She hesitated for a moment. She turned around and walked into the kitchen, but after a few slow minutes of clattering pots and pans, she came back out. She walked out the door, across the porch, down the steps, and onto the sidewalk. It was 11:50. I was crazed! All I could think to do was run after her. I made sure the doors were closed, and I ran as fast as I could behind her. My eyes were so full of tears I could barely see where I was going.

"Please, Grandma, come back. Stop and come back home. I don't know how to lock the door, come back and show me. Please, Grandma, please!"

She acted as if she didn't hear me. She walked on, faster and faster. I could not keep up. Surely it was twelve o'clock.

I stopped and looked back toward the bus stop. I could just make out the bus corner, almost three long blocks from me. As I watched, I saw that big yellow West End bus turn on Horah Street. I was frightened. I looked back toward the end of the street just in time to see Grandma disappearing around the corner of Innes Street.

"Grandma, wait! Aunt Mildred's coming, she's gonna walk with us." I ran to the corner in time to see her walk across the railroad tracks. I was torn now. Was I to stay with my grandma or go back to tell Aunt Mildred what was happening? I turned back, running toward the bus stop. I could just make out the shape of a woman walking down the street carrying a grocery bag in her arms. I recognized that knock-kneed walk of hers: it was Aunt Mildred. I started running toward her, screaming at the top of my voice.

Two streets to cross. I slowed up just before getting to the curb, looked both ways, and took off. By the time I got to Aunt Mildred, she had put the grocery bag in her other arm and was saying to me, "What's wrong with you? Stop crying and tell me now. What is it?"

When I told her she seemed shocked and bewildered, at a loss for words. But she finally got it together and started walking fast. As we passed the house she said, "Stay here and take these things in the house." I watched as she started running in the direction that Grandma had taken.

For two days my grandma was missing. We had everybody looking, including the county sheriff and the city police department. Uncle Nesbert was the one who found her. She was only about two miles from home, walking along the highway. When he found her, she said, "I've been looking for you."

She arrived home tired and exhausted. Her

memory seemed gone completely. Her face was dirty, her shoes were muddy, and she had lost her purse, but she didn't seem to be upset by her ordeal.

I could not believe what I saw. This wasn't the person who had cooked wonderful food, sewn my ripped clothes, cooled my fevered brow, and loved me when it seemed nobody else did. What had happened to our wonderful life? It was no more.

My grandma lived for ten more years in this unusual state, never recognizing us, never seeming to care about anyone or anything, never speaking. We fed her, bathed her, diapered her. Aunt Georgia, Grandma's sister-in-law, once said, "She's living in a Paradise Hell."

Well, that statement made the grown-ups in the family very angry and upset with her. My Aunt Mildred stopped speaking to her. At first I was not sure how I felt about that statement, but I analyzed it and quickly decided it was true. When I became an adult, I realized that Grandma had been suffering from Alzheimer's. I ask you, what is Alzheimer's disease to a victim, if not a Paradise Hell?

In January 1964, I was a freshman at Livingstone College in Salisbury. My Aunt Mildred woke me at half past seven one morning and asked me to follow her. She had something to show me. I followed her into Grandma's bedroom. As I walked through the door and approached her bed, I realized that Grandma had fallen asleep. Her pink flannel gown against the whiteness of the sheet caught my eye. Her long gray braids tied with little black bows rested on her breast. But as I looked at her face, I realized that this was not a normal sleep.

Her face was now calm and smooth. The furrows that had been locked into her brow for years were relaxed and gone. I looked back at Aunt Mildred, waiting for her to say something. Large, glistening tears slowly fell from her eyes. I turned again, touched Grandma's hand, then bent to kiss her face.

My friend was gone.

Br'er Rabbit Goes Hunting

Little girls don't pay any attention to the change of seasons. One day you've got on a big coat with undershirts and long pants and leggings—and the next day, an organdy dress, starched and crisp, thin and cool. I never paid much attention to the seasons. But I did know that when we put on coats, Santa Claus was not far away.

I remember asking Pa about the sounds we could hear in the night. He told me it was gunshots I heard. People were hunting in the woods. In the fall or winter, you could hear those sounds every night.

My uncles would bring rabbits and squirrels and possum and raccoon for Grandma to cook. I never knew exactly what I was eating. It was always meat to me. But Pa would really make over the meals when we had something like that for dinner—something wild.

When I tell the story about Br'er Rabbit going hunting, my mind goes back to those long cool nights out in the country.

It was one of those bright days in the big woods, a day when most animals were working and doing all they could while the sun was shining. But not so for Br'er Rabbit. He woke up that morning feeling lazy.

He walked out to the big road and decided the sun was too hot for him to go any further. So he just set himself beside the road and lay back under a shade tree.

Well, by and by, along came Br'er Bear with a sack in his hand. "Well, howdy, Br'er Rabbit! It's a fine day, don't you think?"

"Howdy, Br'er Bear. It is indeed the finest day I've ever seen. Where are you off to with that towsack?"

"I'm going turkey hunting."

"I was thinking of doing a little hunting myself. But seeing as how you'll be hunting around here, I wouldn't want to take all the turkeys from you."

"I do appreciate that considerably," said Br'er Bear, "and maybe tomorrow will be just as fine a day as today and you can go hunting yourself."

Br'er Rabbit had no more urge to hunt than anything.

He said goodbye to Br'er Bear and lay back under the shade tree for the rest of the day.

By and by, Br'er Bear headed back toward home with a sack full of turkeys. Now, Br'er Rabbit had been sitting there under a tree for a mighty long time, and his stomach was empty. He spotted Br'er Bear coming, and thought how much he'd really enjoy having roast turkey for supper. Br'er Bear didn't see Br'er Rabbit sitting back under the tree, and walked along happy as he could be with that sack full of wild turkeys.

Br'er Rabbit suddenly ran into the woods, then came back out to the road, where he lay down with a stick that looked like an arrow beneath his arm.

Br'er Bear came along and saw Br'er Rabbit lying in the road. He couldn't believe his eyes.

"Lordsey be," said Br'er Bear, "this here's a dead rabbit! I sure could do with a little rabbit stew for supper. If I didn't have a sack already full of turkeys, I'd take me this rabbit." But Br'er Bear just shook his head and walked on.

Br'er Rabbit jumped up and ran as fast as he could through the woods, then back out onto the road, where he put that stick under his arm and lay down on the road again.

Down the road came Br'er Bear, slow and unconcerned.

"Well, do tell," said Br'er Bear. "If it ain't another dead rabbit. There's one back there in the road and one here. Why that's two, and if I didn't have this sack of turkeys, I sure would have rabbit stew for a time. My, my, my," he said, and walked on.

Br'er Rabbit got up and ran as fast as he could through the woods and back out onto the road. He placed the stick beneath his arm and stretched out in the road again.

Down the road came Br'er Bear with his sack of turkeys. He spied Br'er Rabbit on the road.

"Why, ain't this something. Somebody's been shooting a whole heap of rabbits and just leaving them. Here's one here and there's another back there and there's one further back from there. That's enough rabbits for weeks of stew. I won't have to hunt at all if I get them rabbits."

Br'er Bear put his sack of turkeys down so that he could carry those three rabbits. Then he turned and ran back down the road, singing as he went along:

> *Rabbit stew for one.*
> *Rabbit stew for two.*
> *Rabbit stew for me.*
> *Rabbit stew for you.*

Br'er Rabbit jumped up, grabbed that sack of turkeys, and ran as fast as he could through the woods, singing as he went along:

> *Roasted turkeys for one.*
> *Roasted turkeys for two.*
> *Roasted turkeys for me,*
> *And none for you.*

"I fooled you again," laughed Br'er Rabbit, and home he went with his sack of turkeys.

Mammy Bammy
Big Money

For a long time, I had in my mind these words: "Mammy Bammy Big Money, the rabbit witch, is home. What for you here?"

As an adult working in the public library, I searched for these words in children's stories. I knew they were from a story that my grandfather had told me, but I could never remember all of it.

One day in 1992 my Uncle Nesbert, who was then seventy-one, and I were talking about my new project, writing down some of the stories that my granddaddy told. I gave him a short list of titles, and just happened to mention I sure would like to remember all of "Mammy Bammy Big Money."

He closed his eyes and dropped his head as if he were in deep thought, then said, "I believe I remember hearing a story like that. I don't know if I can get it all together, but

I'll try."

This is what he remembered.

Br'er Rabbit had crawled inside a long, hollow log. Br'er Wolf ran from one end of the log to the other trying to get him out. He beat on the log in the middle like a drum. But Br'er Rabbit was pretty far back in the log, and Br'er Wolf couldn't reach him. Soon Br'er Wolf gave up and went away, but Br'er Rabbit stayed inside the log in deep thought.

What had happened to him? This was the third time Br'er Wolf had come that close to catching him. Br'er Bear, Br'er Fox, and Br'er Wolf seemed to have stepped up their pursuit of him, and it looked like it was just a matter of time before they'd have him skinned and cooked.

When Br'er Rabbit arrived home he told his wife, Sis Rabbit, that it was time for him to go on a trip that was quite dangerous. Sis Rabbit packed Br'er Rabbit some food for his trip, some corn bread and sassafras tea. Br'er Rabbit got his walking stick, strapped his food sack to his back, and off he went to call on Mammy Bammy Big Money.

Mammy Bammy Big Money lived in a deep hole on an island in the middle of the swamp. That meant walking many miles to the swamp, boarding a leaky boat, and paddling with half an oar through black water full of snakes and alligators to the island. Br'er

Rabbit made it, but when he arrived, he was shaking like a leaf on a tree.

"Mammy Bammy Big Money, oh, sweet Mammy Bammy Big Money, I've come home in this high grass."

All of a sudden a big puff of gray smoke came rolling out of the ground, and as it did it turned black and disappeared. Then Br'er Rabbit heard from deep down in the hole, "Br'er Rabbit, Br'er Rabbit, is that you? Mammy Bammy Big Money, the rabbit witch, is home. What for you here?"

Br'er Rabbit knew that she didn't make much conversation, so he got right to the point. "I believe I've lost my luck. I'm not as smart as I used to be."

"Well," said she, "let us see. There's Br'er Squirrel in his tree. Go make him move and bring him back to me."

Br'er Rabbit thought about it and emptied his sack of food and picked up two rocks. He put the sack over his head and sat under the tree. Every once in awhile, Br'er Rabbit would hit the rocks together. Every time he'd strike them together, Br'er Squirrel would get curious and move a little closer.

"Who's in the sack, and what are you doing?" yelled Br'er Squirrel.

"I'm crackin' nuts as big as eggs," yelled Br'er Rabbit.

"Well, I like nuts pretty good," said Br'er Squirrel. "Let me help you."

"Come on and get in the sack with me," called out Br'er Rabbit, and Br'er Squirrel jumped in.

When Mammy Bammy Big Money got the sack, she turned it upside down and out ran Br'er Squirrel.

"That was easy as tastin' cake. Now bring me back a coiled up snake," said the rabbit witch.

Br'er Rabbit thought long about this. Then he climbed a tree and cut down a willowy grapevine and tied a slipknot on the end. It wasn't long before he found a snake coiled in the grass.

"Howdy do, Br'er Snake, I was just thinking about you." Br'er Snake stayed still and peeked at Br'er Rabbit through half-closed eyes. He didn't say a word.

"Well, me and Br'er Bear were just speculating 'bout how long you are. Br'er Bear says you're just three feet long, and I say noooo, Br'er Snake is a full-grown four-footer," said Br'er Rabbit.

Br'er Snake had opened his eyes by now. He just kind of grinned as Br'er Rabbit kept talking.

"I would like to prove to Br'er Bear just how long you really are. Would you let me measure you?"

Br'er Snake flicked his tongue in the air and crawled out in a straight-as-a-stick position. Br'er Rabbit dropped that slipknot over his head and tightened it. Then he dragged Br'er Snake back to Mammy Bammy Big Money.

All Br'er Rabbit could see were puffs of black smoke coming through the hole where she lived. But he could hear her saying, "You got plenty sense and a heap of luck. If you get any more it could ruin the world."

Br'er Rabbit went home, skinned Br'er Snake and ate him, and never worried again.

Br'er Rabbit
Pays His Respects

My Uncle James was a very tall, slim, medium brown, gray-eyed, handsome man who dressed sharp and always looked good. He lived in Washington, D.C. and came home to visit Pa and Grandma often. Uncle James was, as I remember, a really good cook. When he came home, my grandmother stepped out of her kitchen and let him take over.

Uncle James was a teaser. He would tease me sometimes until I cried. But he made up for it when he'd pick me up in his arms and apologize for teasing me and then tell me a good story.

Once he came home for a family funeral. I was being my usual self, asking a thousand questions about the day's events. When Uncle James noticed I was annoying Grandma, he picked me up and took me outside under the tree. We sat and ate peanuts and corn candy and that's when I heard the story of how Br'er Rabbit paid his respects.

Br'er Bear and Br'er Fox were always trying to catch Br'er Rabbit in one of his tricks. They had tried outsmartin' him more times than they could remember, but each time Br'er Rabbit came out on top.

One day Br'er Bear and Br'er Fox got a good idea about how they could outsmart Br'er Rabbit.

So Br'er Fox went to Br'er Rabbit's house and knocked on the door. When Br'er Rabbit answered the door, Br'er Fox was crying, "Oh, Br'er Rabbit, I just had to come and tell you the bad news."

Br'er Rabbit looked at Br'er Fox, real suspicious, and said, "Why, Br'er Fox, why are you crying so?"

"Oh, Br'er Rabbit, it's terrible. Poor Br'er Bear, our good friend, has passed on. He's dead," cried Br'er Fox.

"Well," said Br'er Rabbit, "I'm sorry to hear that. What on earth happened to him?"

"Well," said Br'er Fox, "I was stopping over to see him today and I knocked at his door. He never answered. I knew he was home, so I just opened the door and walked in. There he was, lying there in his bed, dead as a doornail."

"I do declare," said Br'er Rabbit. "That beats all I've ever heard. Why, I just saw Br'er Bear yesterday, when we were both hunting on the same land. He didn't seem to be sick or ailing. You sure he's dead?"

Br'er Fox seemed to dry his tears a bit now. "No, I'm not sure, but then I've never seen anyone dead like that before. Maybe you can tell."

Br'er Rabbit and Br'er Fox lit out toward Br'er Bear's home.

Br'er Bear lived in a cave not too far from Br'er Rabbit, so Br'er Fox and Br'er Rabbit didn't have far to walk. As they approached Br'er Bear's cave, Br'er Rabbit noticed Br'er Fox was dropping behind him. "Come on Br'er Fox," said Br'er Rabbit. "It's going to take both of us to tell if he's dead."

Old Br'er Fox fell back some more as Br'er Rabbit walked along ahead of him. Br'er Fox had a big, wide grin on his face 'cause he knew that before too long Br'er Rabbit would be in the stew pot.

When Br'er Rabbit and Br'er Fox opened the door, they could see Br'er Bear all laid out in his bed.

Now Br'er Rabbit realized that there was something wrong. Br'er Fox and Br'er Bear just might be trying to trick him so that they could catch him. Br'er Rabbit had to think fast.

Br'er Fox pretended to cry—"*No! No!*"—and tried to convince Br'er Rabbit that he was really grief-stricken.

"Can you tell, Br'er Rabbit?" asked Br'er Fox. "Can you tell if he's dead? Move on over there close to him so you can see real good."

"I don't think I need go any closer," said Br'er

Rabbit. "I've seen a heap of dead folks. Every one of them did one thing."

"One thing?" asked Br'er Fox.

"One thing," said Br'er Rabbit.

"Is Br'er Bear doing it?" asked Br'er Fox.

"Well, he ain't done it yet," said Br'er Rabbit.

"What is it he's supposed to do," said Br'er Fox, "that he ain't doing?"

"Well," Br'er Rabbit said, "it's just hard to say whether Br'er Bear has passed away or not, 'cause all the dead folks that I have ever seen did a little move that Br'er Bear isn't doing now."

"What move can he do to prove he's dead?" said Br'er Fox.

"I can see that he's laid out. Well, he's still and quiet like he's dead, but he ain't said 'Wa Hoo.'"

"What did you say?" asked Br'er Fox. "He ain't said what?"

"Most dead folks that I knew said 'Wa Hoo.' They sat up good and tall and yelled out 'Wa Hoo.'"

Br'er Fox thought about it and said, "If Br'er Bear is sure enough dead, he should be saying 'Wa Hoo' at any moment now."

Suddenly Br'er Bear sat up on the bed and yelled as loud as he could, "Wa Hoo!"

Br'er Rabbit ran to the door and down the road he went, laughing as loud as he could. "I fooled you again," said Br'er Rabbit. "I fooled you again!"

Br'er Fox and Br'er Bear just stood and watched

as Br'er Rabbit skipped down the road, free as the breeze.

The Legend of Annie Christmas

While working in the great city of New Orleans, I visited the park where the beautiful horsedrawn wagons start up.

I sat one Sunday with the carriage drivers. We talked and told stories to each other. One of the older fellows—one they called Spade—told me the story of Annie Christmas.

The white folks in New Orleans say Annie Christmas was white; the black folks say she was black. So nobody knows for sure what race Annie belonged to, but she was *some* woman.

Annie Christmas was a keelboat pilot on the Mississippi River. She was seven feet tall in her stocking feet, weighed four hundred pounds, and had a fine growth of a mustache on her face. She wore a hat with a red turkey feather sticking from the band, and all who saw it knew not to trifle with Annie.

She was fearless and could beat any man with fist, fire, or knife. Mike Fink, the hero of the Ohio Valley, came to fight Annie once and never returned to New Orleans or the Mississippi River after Annie whipped him.

Annie dressed like a man most of the time, but she would sometimes feel like getting all dressed up, like the women she saw on the riverboats as they sailed down the Mississippi. So one day, Annie bought herself fifteen yards of red satin and sewed herself the prettiest frock you've ever seen. She bought herself a ticket on the *River Queen*. Annie was the talk of the riverboat that night. Her red satin dress was accented by a necklace made from the ears, eyes, and noses that she had chewed or gouged or cut off during her many fights on the river. They say when she died that necklace was twenty feet long!

That night on the *River Queen*, Annie met Charlie, a riverboat gambler and quite a fancy dan. Annie fell head over heels in love with Charlie, and about a year later they were married.

One year later, Annie gave birth to twelve sons. All twelve were born at the same time, and within six years they were all seven feet tall and worked on the river like their mother.

Charlie and Annie often sailed on the riverboats so Charlie could do his gambling there. One night Charlie was playing roulette while Annie looked on.

He played twenty-five dollars on red, leaned forward, and watched as the ball rolled and rested. Red had won. Charlie let it roll again. Five times in a row he won.

Annie begged him to stop. Charlie let it ride ten times in a row. Annie said, "Please, Charlie, please stop. Your luck can't hold out."

Sixteen times the ball fell on red, and the captain realized that Charlie had won ten thousand dollars of the house's money. So he said, "Charlie, you can't play no more." Well, Annie grabbed Charlie by the arm, and as she did, Charlie fell to the floor.

Charlie had been dead for a long time. The riverboat had been playing against a dead man, and the dead man had won every time.

Annie's grief was more than she could bear. She grieved herself to death. When she died, her sons built her a black coffin and put it in a black hearse drawn by twelve black horses. They placed it all on a black barge, cut the ropes of the barge, and let it drift down to the Mississippi under a dark moon.

Now, some folks say when the Mississippi rolls high and it's a dark, dark night, you just might hear the water lapping against Annie Christmas's coffin barge.

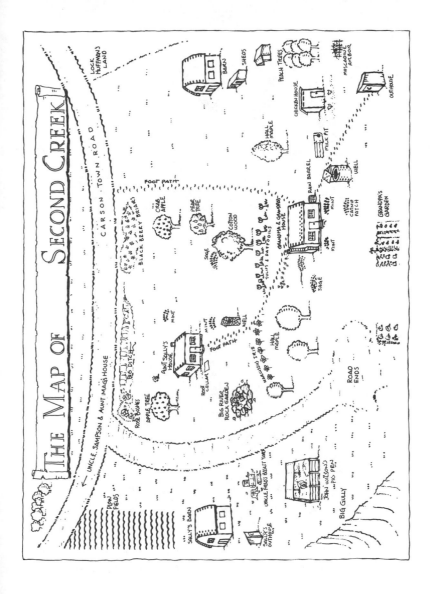

My grandpa, James Mitchell Carson, standing in front of the milk pit - a cold food storage area similar to a root cellar- c. 1945, Second Creek, North Carolina.

The ex-slave, Samuel Mitchell Carson (far right), *seated with people of the Carson Town community, in the late 1920s.*

Left to right: Uncles Leroy, James, William, and Nesbert. This picture was taken after the death of my Aunt Malivia in Chicago, Illinois, in 1967. Uncle Lawrence and Uncle Leonard are missing.

My mother, Mae Troy Carson (center) *with my aunts Edna* (left) *and Malivia, Chicago, Illinois, 1944.*

My aunt, Sally Carson Wilson, standing with (left) Grandpa and another brother, Fred Carson, around 1949.

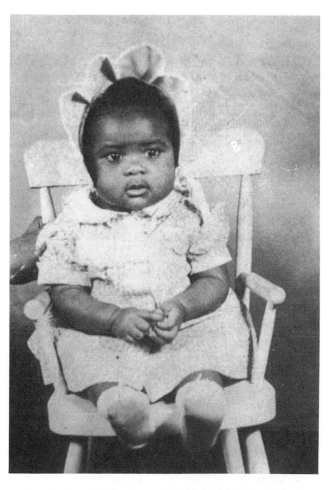

Jacqueline LaVonia Carson: This picture was taken at Stone Studio in Salisbury, North Carolina, May 1946.

My grandmother was sick when this picture was taken, around 1959. The photographer had been with us almost two hours before she decided to smile.

This photo was taken on my eighth birthday. My mother was twenty-eight years old.

My aunt, Mildred Elizabeth Carson, on her high school graduation in 1930.

This picture of my grandma, Ola Hannah Carson, was taken in Chicago, Illinois, on her seventy-fifth birthday, January 1950.

My uncle, Nesbert Carson. When I was little, he'd sing to me, "I'll fly away, Oh Lordy, I'll fly away, when I die, Halleluiah bye and bye, I'll fly away ..." I called that his theme song.

Me, Myself, and I

No doubt you have in your lifetime heard some-one speak of searching for his or her identity. Well, I never had to search. I always knew who I was.

I knew at an early age that I was the great-grand-daughter of a slave named Samuel Mitchell Carson, a teacher and a minister of the Gospel. I also knew that my grandparents were pillars of the community, and that my aunts and uncles were highly respected in their communities by employers and friends.

I was told of the exploits of this slave, my great-grandfather, and of this land that was given him and how it increased in acreage because of his intelligence. My grandparents told me these stories. It seemed they were saying that I must never be anything less than all that I could be for fear of letting my ancestors down.

I wrote my full name on a piece of paper the other day and took a long, long look at it. Jacqueline La-Vonia Carson Seals Torrence. The first two names were given free and clear. Clean and new, unused. The third name, Carson, that was the trick. It was fully loaded. History was packed into it. Not history that you read about in great reference books from the library, but family history. Personal strides, little glories, small triumphs, meaningful successes, and great victories. It was up to me to build on what was already there.

The first twenty years were filled with trial and error—mostly error.

My mother's name was Mae Troy Carson. She was the second youngest of thirteen children. She had a twelfth-grade education. As she marched in the line of high school graduates, she carried an extra burden: me. With her secret intact, she left North Carolina and moved in with her sisters in Chicago, Illinois, hoping to delay the moment of acknowledgment to the whole family.

She was able to confide in her sisters. They persuaded her to give her child to one of them when it was born, and no one back at home in Second Creek would ever have to know her secret. Her sisters Edna and Malivia were both childless. My mother agreed.

On the night of February 11, 1944, Mother was spending the night with her sister Edna on the south side of Chicago, far away from Malivia, who had agreed to take the child and care for it as her own.

I was born in Providence Hospital at 10:00 A.M. on February 12, 1944. My mother took one look at me and decided I was so ugly I might be mistreated if they saw me, so she kept me. I spent the first three months of my life in Chicago. Then I was taken to North Carolina because my Aunt Mildred asked my mother to bring me home so that she could see me.

From the day I arrived, I was home. Although my grandma was angry about my mother's mistake and never let her forget it, I enjoyed the attentions of Aunt Mildred, Grandma, Pa, Aunt Sally, Uncle Nesbert, and all the rest of the family.

My mother often played with me. We made mud pies together. We drank tea and cocktails from make-believe champagne glasses, fried cow pasture daisies for fried eggs, cooked locust leaves for string beans, and picked dockweed for salad greens. She was my playmate. But soon things got too hard for her with my grandma. Every time my mother left home or wanted to go shopping or visiting, my grandma would accuse her of going out to get another baby.

Mother would tell me these stories as I grew up, and as she spoke I'd always see tears form in her eyes. Finally, she left North Carolina, and left me, at my Aunt Mildred's request, with my grandma. Aunt Mildred took care of my financial needs, while Grandma and Grandpa looked after me day and night.

After we moved to Marsh Street in Salisbury, we

stayed with Uncle Nesbert and his wife, Talmadge. Later we moved again to live with Aunt Mildred in her big old two-story house on Lloyd Street. I must have been about five years old, because that was the year I started kindergarten.

Kindergarten! Mrs. Helen Wood was my teacher. Billy Henderson, my next-door neighbor, and I were the same age. We would walk to Miss Helen's house, which was only half a block away, and Miss Helen, Billy, and I would walk about seven blocks to the small Lutheran Church on the corner of Craig and Marsh Streets where Miss Helen taught twenty-four five-year-olds.

Out of Miss Helen's class, two people have become successful doctors, another a head nurse at Johns Hopkins University Hospital, one a college president, one a nationally known storyteller, and three have acquired Ph.Ds. Quite an accomplishment for one teacher!

Miss Helen's husband's name was Mr. J.C. That's what we would call him. Mr. J.C. was a handyman who drove a big, rusted-out Ford panel truck. The back of the truck was big and fat. Billy and I used to laugh between ourselves and make fun of that truck, calling it Mr. J.C.'s old "rusty butt" truck. One day, while we were in school, it started to snow and the snow came down harder and harder. Most of the children had been picked up, but the rest of us didn't have any way to get home. Miss Helen tried to assure us that all would be well, but to a five-year-old who had not seen that much snow and was that far away from home, it was frightening! All of a sudden we heard this awful racket outside the church, and there was Mr. J.C. in his rusty-butt truck.

Mr. J.C. ran into the church calling for Miss Helen. "Get the young'uns ready, Helen, we takin' 'em home."

Mr. J.C. looked like a knight in shining armor and that rusty-butt truck was now a limousine. We were jumping up and down so, Miss Helen could hardly get our coats on. We all climbed into the back of the truck. Billy and I held on to one another. Every time the truck would hit a bump or slide on the ice, something in the back of the truck among Mr. J.C.'s tools and work paraphernalia would fall over—*bounce, knock, bing-a-bang*—and Billy and I would fall over laughing.

Miss Helen rode in the front seat with her head held high. Mr. J.C. drove that truck with his whole body, and every time he'd hit a bump you'd hear him call out, "Watch out, Nellie, just take things easy. Whoa, Nellie, take your time." Mr. J.C. and Miss Helen got all the children home safe and sound. As they stopped to let Billy and me out, Miss Helen smiled and said, "J.C.'s old rusty-butt truck came in handy today, didn't it?"

Billy and I just looked at each other and wondered, how did she know we had laughed at Mr. J.C.'s truck? From that day on I had a healthy respect for Mr. J.C.'s truck. When I'd hear it backfire up the street, I'd say to myself, "Watch out, Nellie, just take things easy."

The first few years of elementary school were enlightening indeed. Life got really complicated. I became aware of my speech problems—or more precisely, my classmates made me aware. They were the ones who laughed every time I opened my mouth. They laughed when I talked, laughed when I walked, and boy, did they have a time if I tried to run ... I was fat, too!

The fifth grade was a trying time in my life. My classmates were just old enough to say cruel, mean things about the way I spoke and about my size. Many days I went home with tearstains on my face—silent tears that never made a sound in my throat but left tracks on my cheeks.

Early that school year, I made up my mind never to speak to anyone again. If I didn't speak, no one could laugh at me. But it didn't quite work out that way. My teacher, Pauline Pharr, did not allow her students to be nonresponsive.

A few days before Halloween, Mrs. Pharr asked us to write "a creative story about Halloween." She then said that after she checked the papers we each would be expected to read our story to the class. Well, to any other fifth-grader that was par for the course, but for me that was like a sentence to death by firing squad. All my shortcomings would be on display. I was so overwhelmed by this I started crying quietly in my seat as my classmates wrote away.

After some time, Mrs. Pharr came over to ask me why I wasn't writing like my fellow classmates. By this time the whole class had figured out what my dilemma was, and some of them were laughing. They were totally out of control. Mrs. Pharr must have sensed that I was feeling hurt and scared, anticipating what I would have to do.

She suggested that I write the very best story I could and she would read it aloud for me. With her encouragement, I wrote a good story, and sure enough, she read it.

Mrs. Pharr had unearthed my writing ability. That changed my feelings about myself, and my new-found talent lessened my classmates' ridicule of me. In later years, there would be corrective dental work, but I have always felt that my healing began that day.

I watched my grandma change, with little understanding of just what was happening to her. I saw her struggling with being relocated, and thought the reason for her health problems was simply her forced move away from her beloved Second Creek home to the town. Later I found out there were others in the family who felt the same way, and they tried to help.

Uncle Nesbert would take her to visit Aunt Sally on Sundays to talk to the other relatives who lived out there. She would pick broomsage in the fall, and roots and barks and all the things she needed for her medicines. But that did not make her happy. Usually on the way back home she was quiet, rarely volunteering a conversation.

Grandma finally stopped going to the old homeplace after Aunt Sally died. I think it just made her too sad. She would often ask Uncle Nesbert, Aunt Mildred, and Uncle Will what was going on out there, but when they answered it didn't seem to mean much to her.

It was about this time that money started getting really tight for Aunt Mildred. She was trying to get the land taxes for Second Creek paid, for Grandma's sake, but they had gotten behind and the land was about to be sold. She sought the advice of a local lawyer who suggested that the buildings be removed to lower the taxes. This would mean taking down the house, the shed, and the barn. Aunt Mildred located a man who had a bulldozer who would do the work of pushing the house and sheds down at a reasonable price.

I remember the day very well. It was a Saturday, in the spring, and the daffodils, tulips, and other flowers that grew in rows in the front and side yards were in full bloom.

We got Uncle Nesbert to drive us to the country. As we drove past Aunt Sally's house, we could see that the man and his bulldozer were already there. Uncle Nesbert parked the car in Aunt Sally's yard. It felt strange to me when Uncle Nesbert drove down the road and into Aunt Sally's yard. I looked up toward the house half-expecting to see Aunt Sally come out on the porch and greet us, though Aunt Sally had passed away and the house was empty. We got out of the car and walked the old path toward Grandma's house. I was filled to the brim with excitement! I just couldn't walk that path—I ran. I ran to the rows of flowers and started picking a handful. These flowers, I thought, would please Grandma, who loved them so much.

I walked and picked, and then I noticed that Aunt Mildred and Uncle Nesbert and the man with the bulldozer had gone into the house. I was curious and wanted to know what they were up to. As I entered the house I heard them talking. The bulldozer operator suggested that all the stuff in the cabinets, like glass and breakable things, be removed so that his job wouldn't be so dangerous. I looked around. There were bits and pieces of my grandma's life everywhere.

She'd left dishes, bowls, glasses, cookware, crockery, and many other things that had meant so much to her. She'd left them because they told her she would not have room for these things when she moved.

There were drawers filled with kitchen linens and there were still many pieces of furniture left in the house. I watched as Aunt Mildred and Uncle Nesbert took three tin washtubs and emptied cabinets and drawers of their breakable contents into the tubs. I stayed out of the way, but as one drawer after another was opened and slammed closed again, I saw something that I wanted. Yet if I stopped to get it, I just might miss something else. Thinking I would return later to retrieve my treasure, I continued through the house with my aunt and uncle.

When they finished, the tubs were carried to the big gully and dumped. Down the hill rolled the great big bowls in which Grandma had mixed wonderful cakes and bread, sliced peaches and apples, and shelled peas. Down went glasses that had held tea and milk and sweet, sweet lemonade and cool water. Gone forever were the glass bowls that had held watermelon rind pickles, bread-and-butter pickles made with onions and vinegar. As they hit the bottom of the gully I could hear them break and crack and shatter.

Then I heard someone call my name. It was Uncle Nesbert telling me to go up the hill toward Aunt Sally's house. Aunt Mildred was already there and the bulldozer was on the way. I stood beside Aunt Mildred and watched the big piece of machinery toiling its way toward the house. My eyes took one more long look toward Grandma's place. I suddenly remembered the treasured object that I had meant to retrieve from the house. I ran down the hill, into the yard, onto the porch, and through the house to the kitchen. I pulled open one of the drawers, grabbed my treasured item, and turned to run out again.

As I reached the door, my Aunt Mildred grabbed me. Although she was yelling and screaming, I could barely hear what she was saying. I watched her mouth until it all came together.

"What in God's name are you doing? Do you realize that you could have been killed?"

Too scared to move or speak, I lifted my treasure and handed it to her. She was silent for just a moment as she unfolded it.

"You mean to tell me," she said softly, "that this old, rotten, faded-out, ragged apron is the reason you almost got yourself killed? Do you realize that bull-dozer was only fifteen or twenty feet from this house? That man couldn't see you, and he could barely hear me yelling for him to stop. Would you please explain to me what you were doing?"

I waited before I spoke. I wasn't sure she really meant for me to speak, but the look on her face meant speak now or get yelled at again.

I said, "I just wanted Grandma's apron."

As we moved off the porch and Aunt Mildred pulled me back up the path, I thought, *If she only knew*. To her, that apron was an old feed sack, a rotten, faded rag. To me, it was a magic cloak.

In the evening when Grandma's work was all

done, she would pick up the hem of her apron and tuck it into the waistband. That was always her way of saying, *Work's all done for today.* We sat on the porch or in front of the fire. Sometimes on the porch late in the evening, the mosquitoes would really get tough on me. I would jump and squirm and scratch. My grandma would pull the apron off and wrap it around me. The mosquitoes didn't bite anymore! That apron was like a lead jacket. They couldn't penetrate it. It was magic!

In the mornings, Grandma would follow the hens into the big gully where they laid eggs. She knew where the nest was and would lift the hem of her apron, tie it in a knot, and make a basket to carry the eggs. It was magic!

When Pa came back from town, I'd jump off the porch and run to meet him. I almost always fell, stumbling over my own feet, getting dirt and sand in the scrapes and cuts. Grandma would hear me crying. She would lift the end of her apron, dip it into fresh, cool water, wash my wounds, and hold the cold cloth over it. When she took it off, the bleeding had stopped and I was no longer in pain. It was magic!

Sometimes at church there would be a dinner after the service. While Grandma prepared her food for serving, other people found time to tease me about my speech impediment. They would always laugh and embarrass me. I'd run and hide under Grandma's apron and that made me invisible so they couldn't see me anymore. That apron was truly magic!

Now my aunt was saying it was only an old, rotten rag. That's what it was to her. Not to me.

I was a child then but I'm all grown up now. I know right from wrong, day from night, and all that stuff in the middle. I still own my Grandma's apron. I know it's not magic. But sometimes when life gets to be totally confusing, when my mind can't make complex decisions, I find the box where her apron stays and I wrap it around my face and smell deep down inside of it and remember the times when it *was* magic.

When I entered ninth grade, I met another guardian angel. My teacher, Mrs. Abna Lancaster, took an interest in me. She worked with me day and night and Saturdays to change my speech. She always said she never taught school, she taught students.

One day she said to me, "My dear, you are fat." But then she continued. "But I want you to stand up straight and be proud of the body the Lord gave you. Look people in the eye the way you look at me."

With influences like Mrs. Pharr and Mrs. Lancaster—not to mention a librarian named Corine Thomas and all my teachers from kindergarten to college—it is no wonder that I became interested in being a librarian. Eventually I worked as a reference librarian in High Point, North Carolina. One day it snowed, and the staff storyteller wasn't able to get in. But somehow the children were! My boss told me to find some way to entertain the children—read them a book or show them a film or something. Well, I told the children a mountain story from Richard Chase's *Grandfather Tales,* and they loved it. They asked me to tell it again, and I did. And that's how I got started in storytelling.

A few years later, I was hired to perform in a school in Atlanta. The organizers got upset when they learned I planned to tell an Uncle Remus story. The principal said, "I wish you wouldn't. We are trying to teach these children pride."

Now, to me, those old animal stories convey philosophies, values, attitudes in a way that preaching never can. So I said, "Honey, you don't have any pride unless you know where you come from."

The Wonderful Tar Baby

The Tar Baby story was my Uncle Nesbert's tale. He could make Br'er Bear and Br'er Fox into the meanest critters when he told this story.

I remember my mother and me making a tar baby out of mud one day when she was visiting from Chicago. I was busy sifting the red dirt in the road when she walked out from the house and sat down in the dirt with me. Well, I was kind of surprised because Pa and Grandma never played with me like that.

My mother got a bucket of water and showed me how to make mudpies and cakes. The tar baby creation was my idea, though it soon turned into a red mud baby. It dried and sat on the side of the road for a long time. One day we had a hard rainstorm and that was the end of it.

Uncle Nesbert and I would drive by the site in his car and he would say, "Ol' Tar Baby, he just sit there, he don't say nothing."

"Say that again, Uncle Nes," I'd plead, "say that

again!"

Br'er Fox and Br'er Bear had been mighty close to catchin' Br'er Rabbit, time and time again, but Br'er Rabbit had outsmarted them more times than a tree's got leaves.

The closest they ever came to catching him was the day that Br'er Fox and Br'er Bear were down by the tar pit thinking on how they could get Br'er Rabbit for sure.

It was Br'er Fox who came up with the idea of the tar baby. They worked all day a-fixin' and a-fixin', till finally they fashioned a piece of tar that looked just like a tar baby. They put a hat and a coat on the critter, and set him on the side of the road. Then they lay back in the bush, never made a sound.

By and by Br'er Rabbit came strolling along the road, acting like he was king of the world.

He walked on till he spied the tar baby sitting on the side of the road. So Br'er Rabbit, he hauled off and said, "Howdy-do?"

Well, the tar baby, he didn't say nothing. Br'er Fox and Br'er Bear, they lay real quiet in the bush.

"Morning, its a fine day!"

The tar baby, he didn't say nothing, and Br'er Fox and Br'er Bear, they lay quiet.

"Round here, we's all real polite and we speaks when we's spoken to. I'm gonna give you a chance to be polite."

Well, the tar baby didn't say nothing and Br'er Fox and Br'er Bear lay low in the bush. Br'er Rabbit was getting madder and madder.

"If you're hard of hearin', I can speak louder. But I think you're just plain downright disrespectful and you need somebody to teach you some manners. Now when I speak this time, I wants you to speak back. Howdy-do!" he hollered.

The tar baby, he still didn't say nothing, and Br'er Fox and Br'er Bear, they lay quiet.

"Well, this is most distressing," said Br'er Rabbit. "A little lesson-learning for you is what I've got to do. If you don't say howdy when I say howdy I'm gonna rare back and bust wide open. Now I say howdy."

The tar baby, he didn't say a word, and Br'er Rabbit drew way back with his fist, and *whip!* He gave him a slap right on the side of his head. Well, this is just where Br'er Rabbit up and spilled the salt box, 'cause when he slapped the tar baby his right fist just stuck to the side of the tar baby's face.

The tar baby didn't say one word. Br'er Fox and Br'er Bear nearly fell out of the bush, they were laughing so hard.

"Now look here, if you don't turn my hand loose I'm gonna whack you once with my other hand." With that, Br'er Rabbit hauled off and slapped the tar baby with his left hand. That hand stuck.

Tar baby was still quiet.

Br'er Fox and Br'er Bear were beside themselves with glee.

"Turn me loose, turn me loose, or I will kick the stuffin's out of you!" said Br'er Rabbit.

The tar baby never said a word. He just held on to Br'er Rabbit good and tight. Then Br'er Rabbit reared back and *wap!* He lost the use of both feet to the tar baby.

Tar baby, he was still quiet.

Br'er Fox and Br'er Bear were just about bent half-double.

Br'er Rabbit started steaming out of both ears. He was madder than a wet hen.

"You beginning to bother me something fierce. I'm getting ready to do something that you will surely regret. I'm gonna take my head and butt you to the other side of the sun!"

Then Br'er Rabbit took his head and butted the tar baby. Now his head was stuck to the tar baby.

Out of the bush came Br'er Fox and Br'er Bear walking along as innocent as babes in arms.

"Well, if it ain't Br'er Rabbit. Seems like you's all tied up there. Seein' as how you so indisposed, you should be going to my house for dinner," said Br'er Fox.

Br'er Fox and Br'er Bear was laughing so hard they rolled all over the ground.

"Going for dinner," said Br'er Bear. "We gonna have him for dinner."

"I 'spect I got you this time, Br'er Rabbit," says Br'er Fox. "You been sporting round here like you was king of the county. Nobody but your own self got you in this fix. I'm gonna build me the hottest brush fire that's ever been built and barbecue you till you done."

Br'er Rabbit figured he was in bad trouble so he talked real humble.

"I don't care what you do with me, Br'er Fox. Just don't fling me in the briar patch."

"It's just too much trouble to build a fire. I just may find me the tallest tree in the woods and hang you till you dead," whispered Br'er Fox.

"Hang me, hang me high as you please, just don't fling me in the briar patch," pleaded Br'er Rabbit.

"Say, Br'er Bear," said Br'er Fox. "We don't want to have to find no good strong rope, do we? Why don't we just drown you?"

"Drown me, drown me way down deep, but please don't fling me in the briar patch."

"Well, I don't reckon we could do that so easily, 'cause there ain't much water round here to speak of. I believe I'll just skin you."

"Skin me, Br'er Fox, snatch out my eyeballs, tear my hair out, yank my ears out by the roots, cut off my legs and tear off my tail, but whatever you do, don't fling me in that briar patch!" cried Br'er Rabbit.

Br'er Fox wanted to do Br'er Rabbit in, the easiest way he knew how. So he grabbed him, snatched him off the tar baby by the hind legs, and slung him way over deep into the briar patch. Well there was much yelling and screaming and moaning going on when Br'er Rabbit hit the bushes in the briar patch. Br'er Fox and Br'er Bear nearly busted their sides laughing at the plight Br'er Rabbit was in.

Br'er Fox and Br'er Bear laid out for a long time, waitin' and watchin'. After a while Br'er Fox heard someone laughing and calling to him. He looked up, and there on the hill on the other side of the briar patch was Br'er Rabbit, sitting with his hands on his knees, yellin' at the top of his voice.

"Born and bred in a briar patch, born and bred. Can get in and get out quicker than you can say Jack Robinson. I fooled you again!"

Elvira and Henry

In 1988 I received the Annie Glenn Award, which is given to professional people who have overcome a speech or hearing problem and incorporate their earlier disability in their profession. The weeks that preceded the award ceremony gave me time to get my acceptance speech written.

I thought about the years that I suffered the most with my speech—the years of elementary school when the children laughed at me because I could not speak well. I thought about Mrs. Pharr, my fifth-grade teacher, and the scary story she had gently persuaded me to write for Halloween. I had been too frightened to get up in front of the class and read it, but she promised me if I would write it, she would read it for me. That turned everything around for me.

These days I tell a lot of scary stories in performance. The story of Elvira and Henry is a favorite with my audiences.

Many years ago in Piedmont, North Carolina, there lived Elvira and Henry. One day Elvira's sister was feeling a bit poorly and asked if Elvira would come over and see about her.

Now the little town where Elvira's sister lived was quite a ways away. It was wintertime, and Elvira and Henry hitched up the old mule and went on over. They stayed about two nights, and then old Henry said he was anxious to get back home. Elvira wanted to stay one more night.

Henry said, "Elvira, I've got to take care of my critters. Now let's go home."

"Oh," Elvira said, "all right, Henry." They got in the wagon.

But just then the weather turned mighty bad. Why, it started to snow, and the snow turned into sleet, and the sleet turned into icicles on Elvira's nose because there was no top on the wagon.

Elvira kept yelling, "Henry, it's cold out here! My nose is cold and my toes is cold and my stomach's empty. Why in the world would you try and get home tonight?"

And Henry said, "*Kkkkkk*, get up there, mule. Be quiet, Elvira."

"Oh, Henry," she said, "why in the world would you make me sit in this old wagon? I'm tired and cold. I'll tell you what, Henry, at the next house let's stop and see if the folks will let us sleep in their barn or maybe sleep in front of their fireplace, so I don't freeze to death."

"And I want to get home," said Henry. *"Kkkkkk,* get up there, mule."

Just as they rounded a curve, there along the side of the road was a great big house. Well, it was almost midnight, but all the lights in the house were on, so Elvira said, "Henry, Henry, there's a place. Let's stop there, let's stop there."

"But I don't know who lives there."

"Oh I know it," Elvira said, "but let's just stop."

"Oh, all right."

So Henry pulled the mule to a screeching halt and said, "Whoa there, mule," and Elvira stood up and she said, "I'm gonna go in here and ask these folks if we can spend the night in their barn. You find somewhere to put that mule for the night."

"Oh, all right. *Kkkkkk,* get up there, mule."

Elvira walked over the porch and over to the door and knocked: *boom, boom, boom.*

From way back in the back of the house she heard a voice say, "Come in," so she turned the rusty doorknob and pushed the big door open. It made a loud creaking sound, for its hinges were rusty too.

She stepped inside and called, "How do?," but nobody said a word. She tried again. "Hello, anybody home?"

Nobody said a word.

Once more she called, "Hello, anybody home?"

Still nobody said a word, so she walked quickly

down the hallway, crying, "Hello, hello!"

Suddenly she was in the dining room. *Oh my,* she thought to herself. *Look at the food!*

She walked over to the table, which held a big juicy turkey, a huge pan of hot rolls, and a great big pot of coffee. She grabbed a cup and poured herself some coffee, but just as she lifted it to take a sip, she looked over the cup's rim and saw another door.

"Hello," Elvira said in the door's direction, but again nobody said a word, so she quickly opened the door and stepped inside.

All around the room were shelves and shelves of books, and at the back of the room was a huge fireplace with a great big fire. In front of it were two large, comfortable chairs, and in front of each chair was a pair of nice, warm slippers.

Elvira ran over, pulled off her shoes, and tested one of the pairs. Those slippers fit just right. She settled herself in one of the chairs, lifted the cup of coffee to her lips—and remembered Henry.

"Henry, get in here!" she called.

And that's when she heard it—footsteps coming toward the room, one by one. She knew they weren't Henry's, because Henry always dragged his feet when he walked.

The footsteps stopped just in back of her chair, and a voice said, "Good evening, madam."

She turned around, and standing there was a very handsomely dressed gentleman. He wore tall, black leather boots and a fancy frock-tailed coat, as they called them in those days. There was just one thing wrong with him: though he could speak, he had no head.

"Do not worry, madam. I will not harm you," he said.

And Elvira said, "Oh! Who are you talking to? Oh!"

"Madam," he replied, "so many years ago there were visitors in my home, just as you and your husband are tonight. They needed good hot food to eat and a nice warm bed to sleep in, which I provided for them. But because I would not tell where I kept my gold, they killed me and buried my head in one part of the cellar and my body in another part. I've kept this house alive and well, hoping that some day two nice people would come by and help me get myself together again."

"I don't know anything about finding anybody's head," Elvira exclaimed.

Just then, Henry came in. "Brrr," he said. "It's cold out there. I nearly froze to death! But we sure enough found somewhere to spend the … Uh oh! Who … who … who is that?" Henry gaped at the headless man.

"Henry," answered Elvira, "this is the man who owns this house."

"How do you know?"

"He told me."

"He told you. What did he tell you with?"

"Why, with his mouth."

"I don't see a mouth—I don't even see a head. How did he tell you?"

"Henry," she said, "if you'll be quiet he'll tell you too."

Sure enough, the headless man told the story all over again. Henry wanted to know what the man expected *him* to do about it.

"Sir, do you see that door?" he asked. "Down the stairway, sir, you will find the cellar. Beneath the cellar floor somewhere you will find my head. If you will dig and find my head and put it back on my shoulders, I can rest for eternity and I'll never bother you again."

So Henry walked to the door and opened it, but then quickly slammed it and turned around.

"It's dark down there!"

"Oh, do not worry," said the headless man. "I shall provide light for you." With that, he stepped over to the fireplace, lifted one hand into the air, placed the other hand in the fire, and lit one of his fingers. He removed the finger from his hand and gave it to Henry, who said, "Oh, thank you."

He did the same with the other hand: lifted the burnt hand high in the air, lit the end of the finger on that other hand, removed it, and handed it to Elvira. She thanked him.

Elvira and Henry took the strange candles downstairs, where they found picks and shovels, and they dug all night. Finally, just before the sun rose, they climbed back up the stairs with the old man's head and placed it back on his body.

Just before he disappeared for good, the man said, "I thank you for helping me get myself together again. As a reward, I want you to have this house and all the land around it. If you will dig in back of the old oak tree, you'll find the gold that I protected for so many years. It is yours. I'll never bother you again."

And that's what happened. He went away, and Elvira and Henry lived happily ever after.

Br'er Possum's Dilemma

When I was in high school, my best friend promised for months to buy me a sweater. "I'm going to get you that sweater for Christmas," she told me. "I've put it in layaway." Her mother was a teacher, and her father was a professional band director. They had money, and I knew that she could afford to buy me the sweater.

Then she took me shopping downtown and showed me a bracelet and ring that she wanted. Since she had promised me the sweater, I knew that I had to give her something just as nice. The bracelet and ring cost twenty-five dollars, and I begged Aunt Mildred to help me buy it for my friend for Christmas. We were poor, and Aunt Mildred refused.

"But I've got to get that bracelet for her!" I insisted.

Aunt Mildred just said, "I know her and I know her mama, and she's not goin' to get you any sweater. She's just talkin'."

I spent nights awake wondering where I was going to

get the money to buy that jewelry, and finally I persuaded my Uncle Nesbert to give me twenty-five dollars. I bought the bracelet and ring.

Christmas came, and I couldn't wait to get my sweater. But the day was almost over, and I hadn't heard from my friend. So I called her house and learned that her father had taken her to South Carolina, but she'd be back soon. And sure enough, when my friend returned home to Salisbury, she called me.

"I'm back home, and I'm comin' to see you with your Christmas present."

I said, "That's great, 'cause I've got your present, too."

But when she walked into my house, I didn't see a box. I looked at her, puzzled.

She said, "I've got your gift right here."

And from her purse, she pulled a little box and gave it to me. I ripped it open, and instead of the sweater, I found rocks glued to a piece of paper—something you could buy for fifty cents.

I gave her the bracelet and ring, and when she left I started to cry. But Aunt Mildred took me into her arms and said, "I warned you of her nature." Then she told me this story.

Back in the days when the animals could talk, there lived ol' Br'er Possum. He was a fine fellow. Why, he never liked to see no critters in trouble. He was always helpin' out, a-doin' something for others.

Every night, ol' Br'er Possum climbed into a persimmon tree, hung by his tail, and slept all night long. And each morning, he climbed out of the tree and walked down the road to sun himself.

One morning as he walked, he came to a big hole in the middle of the road. Now, ol' Br'er Possum was kind and gentle, but he was also nosy, so he went over to the hole and looked in. All at once, he stepped back, because lying in the bottom of that hole was ol' Br'er Snake with a brick on his back.

Br'er Possum said to himself, "I best get on out of here, 'cause ol' Br'er Snake is mean and evil and low-down, and if I get to staying around him, he just might get to bitin' me."

So, Br'er Possum just went on down the road. But Br'er Snake had seen Br'er Possum.

"Help me, Br'er Possum!"

Br'er Possum stopped and turned around. He said to himself, "That's ol' Br'er Snake a-callin' me. What do you reckon he wants?"

Well, ol' Br'er Possum was kindhearted, so he went back down the road to the hole, stood at the edge, and looked down at Br'er Snake.

"Was that you a-callin' me? What do you want?"

Br'er Snake looked up and said, "I've been down here in this hole for a mighty long time with this brick on my back. Won't you help get it off of me?"

Br'er Possum thought a minute. "Now listen here, Br'er Snake. I knows you. You's mean and evil and low-down, and if I was to get down in that hole and get to liftin' that brick off of your back, you wouldn't do nothin' but bite me."

Ol' Br'er Snake just hissed. "Maybe not. Maybe not. Maaaaaaaybe not."

Br'er Possum said, "I ain't sure 'bout you at all. I just don't know. You're a-goin' to have to let me think about it."

So ol' Br'er Possum thought—he thought high, and he thought low—and just as he was thinkin', he looked up into a tree and saw a dead limb a-hangin' down. He climbed into the tree, broke off the limb, and climbed down. He reached into the hole with that ol' stick and pushed that brick off of Br'er Snake's back. Then he took off down the road.

Br'er Possum thought he was away from ol' Br'er Snake when all at once he heard something.

"Help me, Br'er Possum!"

Br'er Possum said, "Oh no, that's him again."

But being kindhearted, Br'er Possum turned around, went back to the hole, and stood at the edge.

"Br'er Snake, was that you a-callin' me? What do you want now?"

Ol' Br'er Snake looked up from the hole and hissed.

"I've been down here for a mighty long time, and I've gotten a little weak, and the sides of this ol' hole are too slick for me to climb. Do you think you can lift me out of here?"

Br'er Possum thought.

"Now, you just wait a minute. If I was to get down into that hole and lift you out of it, you wouldn't do nothin' but bite me."

Br'er Snake hissed.

"Maybe not. Maybe not. Maaaaaaaybe not."

Br'er Possum said, "I just don't know. You're a-goin' to have to give me time to think about this."

So ol' Br'er Possum thought. And as he thought, he just happened to look down there in that hole and see that ol' dead limb. He pushed the limb underneath ol' Br'er Snake and he lifted him out of the hole, way up into the air, and threw him into the high grass.

Br'er Possum took off a-runnin' down the road.

Well, he thought he was away from ol' Br'er Snake when all at once he heard something.

"Help me, Br'er Possum!"

Br'er Possum thought, "That's him again."

But being so kindhearted, he turned around, went back to the hole, and stood there a-lookin' for Br'er Snake. Br'er Snake crawled out of the high grass just as slow as he could, stretched himself out across the road, rared up, and looked at ol' Br'er Possum.

Then he hissed. "I've been down there in that ol' hole for a mighty long time, and I've gotten a little cold 'cause the sun didn't shine. Do you think you could put me in your pocket and get me warm?"

Br'er Possum said, "Now you listen here, Br'er Snake. I knows you. You's mean and evil and low-down, and if I put you in my pocket you wouldn't do nothin' but bite me."

Br'er Snake hissed.

"Maybe not. Maybe not. Maaaaaaaybe not."

"No, siree, Br'er Snake. I knows you. I just ain't a-goin' to do it."

But just as Br'er Possum was talking to Br'er Snake, he happened to get a real good look at him. He was a-lyin' there lookin' so pitiful, and Br'er Possum's great big heart began to feel sorry for ol' Br'er Snake.

"All right," said Br'er Possum. "You must be cold. So just this once I'm a-goin' to put you in my pocket."

So ol' Br'er Snake coiled up just as little as he could, and Br'er Possum picked him up and put him in his pocket.

Br'er Snake lay quiet and still—so quiet and still that Br'er Possum even forgot that he was a-carryin' him around.

But all of a sudden, Br'er Snake commenced to crawlin' out, and he turned, faced Br'er Possum, and hissed.

"I'm a-goin' to bite you."

Br'er Possum said, "Now, wait a minute. Why are you a-goin' to bite me? I done took that brick off your back, I got you out of that hole, and I put you in my pocket to get you warm. Why are you a-goin' to bite me?"

Br'er Snake hissed.

"You knowed I was a snake before you put me in your pocket."

And when you're minding your own business and you spot trouble, don't ever trouble trouble till trouble troubles you.

Br'er Rabbit
Outsmarts the Frogs

My best audience has always been my daughter, Lori. She was there when I told my first stories at the High Point Public Library. When I was trying to succeed as a full-time professional storyteller and times got tough, she always said to me, "Don't worry. I'll listen to your stories."

Every evening when I tucked her into bed and tried reading her a story, she would wrap her feet in her bed covers and put them on top of my book. "Don't read any more. Tell me a story."

Well, one night she said to me, "Tell me where I come from."

I thought for a moment. "Do you want the truth or a fairy tale?"

"A fairy tale," she said.

I was relieved, and I began to tell her this story:

One day, I read in the newspaper that there were babies on sale at the hospital. The babies were overstocked and were going cheap. I knew how much babies normally cost, and since I didn't have a lot of money, I hurried off to the big sale.

I looked at all of the babies. Some were white, some black, some yellow, some brown. They were all real cute, but I didn't see a single baby that I truly liked.

So finally, I told the clerk in the baby shop that I didn't see anything that I wanted. "Do you have any babies in the stockroom?" I asked, hopefully.

She whispered, "Well, we've got one baby in the stockroom that we've never been able to sell. We took it out of stock because we didn't think anybody would buy it."

And I said, "What's wrong with it?"

"Well," she said, "it has a little mole on its bottom. I'll bring it out and let you see it."

So out of a tattered, old shoe box came this beautiful little baby with a tiny mole on its bottom—a mole that was in the shape of a lovely little star.

My daughter kept asking, "Was it me? Was it me? Was it me?"

I told her, "Out of all of those little babies, I liked you the best. And I brought you home with me."

Lori, satisfied with my story, soon fell off to sleep. But the next day, I received a call from Lori's teacher. She got right to the point. "Mrs. Torrence, if you're going to teach your daughter the facts of life," she suggested, "I have a book here I'd like you to read."

Lori is now grown, and even today when she brings a new friend to the house for a visit, she always introduces me and then says, "Tell her about the shoe box." And I tell that little tale again and again, and the story still lives—even today.

I've told Lori countless other stories, but the one she enjoys the most has always been "Br'er Rabbit Outsmarts the Frogs"—a story my grandma told me.

Ol' Br'er Rabbit lived near the pond, and he was a good fisherman. Every morning he'd drop his hook into the pond, and five or ten minutes later he'd have about fifteen or twenty fish layin' right there on the bank. He was a *good* fisherman.

But Br'er Rabbit had a friend named Br'er Raccoon—he called him Br'er Coon for short—and Br'er Coon couldn't fish at all. He didn't like fish; he liked frogs. But the frogs didn't care too much for Br'er Coon.

Every morning, Br'er Coon got his sack, headed down to the river, filled that ol' sack with frogs, dragged it home, and threw it up on the porch. His wife would see that sack full of frogs and she'd say, "Wooooooo, hee, hee, hee! Frogs!" She liked frogs, too. Br'er Coon and his wife were eatin' up the frog population.

Well, sir, the frogs finally called a big meeting.

"What are we a-goin' to do about Br'er Coon

catchin' us?" asked one of the frogs.

They talked for hours, and finally decided they needed a lookout frog to sit on the bank of the pond and watch for Br'er Coon.

They needed a frog with big eyes to see him when he was a-comin', big ears to hear him when he was a-comin', and a big mouth to warn them when he got there. The only frog that had those qualifications was the bullfrog, and they sent him down to the bank to watch. When Br'er Coon got within a half mile of the river, the bullfrog saw him, heard him, and then he commenced to warnin'.

"Heeeeeeere he comes. Heeeeeeere he comes. Heeeeeeere he comes."

And the little frogs would echo what the bullfrog had said. "Here he comes. Here he comes. Here he comes."

By the time Br'er Coon got to the pond, all of the frogs were in the water—and Br'er Coon couldn't swim. So as the days went by, it started gettin' real slim at home for ol' Br'er Coon. The food was goin' quickly, and try as he might, Br'er Coon wasn't re-plenishing it.

His wife said, "Where's the frogs? Don't you know that we could starve to death? You'd better go out there and catch some frogs!"

And Br'er Coon answered, "Now, wait a minute. Them frogs has done got too wild to catch. I done been down there and every time I come within a half mile, all you can hear is, 'Here he comes. Here he comes. Here he comes.' And I can't catch 'em."

Well, that made her so mad she went to the corner, got the broomstick, and hit him on the head.

"Ooooooohhhh," Br'er Coon cried. "Why'd you do that?"

"We're a-goin' to starve to death. Now you get out of here and find them frogs."

He said, "Now, I done told you—"

"You want me to hit you on the other side?"

"All right. I'm a-goin', I'm a-goin', I'm a-goin'."

Well sir, Br'er Coon left the next morning before the sun came up. He had his ol' sack, and he was walkin' down the road talkin' to himself. "I can't catch them frogs. I done tried. All I hear is 'Here he comes. Here he comes. Here he comes.'"

When he looked up, ol' Br'er Rabbit was comin' toward him. Br'er Rabbit saw his friend and said, "Howdy there, Br'er Coon. How you a-doin'?"

Br'er Coon said, "I ain't doin' too well."

Br'er Rabbit said, "Why, you looks right down in the mouth."

Br'er Coon said, "It ain't my mouth I'm down in. You see this knot on my head?"

"Yeah," Br'er Rabbit said. "Where'd you get it?"

"My wife gave it to me with the broomstick. I can't catch them frogs. I done tried."

"Wait a minute," Br'er Rabbit said. "There's a thousand frogs on one side of that river alone. Why can't you catch 'em?"

He said, "Every time I get within half a mile of the river, all you can hear is 'Here he comes. Here he comes. Here he comes.' And when I get there, they're all in the water and I can't catch 'em."

Br'er Rabbit said, "You need a plan to catch them frogs."

Br'er Coon said, "I don't know nothin' about no plan."

Br'er Rabbit said, "That's all right. You done come to the right place. I'm the best planner that ever planned a plan. I just got to think one up for you."

So, Br'er Rabbit tossed his string of fish that he had caught over a limb on a tree, sat down in the middle of the road on his hind legs, and pricked his ears up in the air. He scratched one ear with one hind leg, and he scratched that other ear with his other hind leg. Then all of a sudden he jumped up and said, "Wooooooo, hee, hee, hee! I've got you a plan."

Br'er Coon said, "What is it?"

"This here's your plan," said Br'er Rabbit. "Go down to the river. When you get to the river, fall dead."

Br'er Coon said, "Do what?"

Br'er Rabbit said, "Ssshhhhhhh. Go down to the river. When you get to the river, fall dead."

Br'er Coon said, "But I don't want to die."

Br'er Rabbit said, "Ssshhhhhhh. I don't mean die. I mean play dead."

Br'er Coon said, "Whew, that's better. So I play dead, but what do I do after that?"

Br'er Rabbit said, "You don't do nothin'. You just lie there. Lie there until I tell you when to move."

"Hee, hee, hee," Br'er Coon said. "I don't know what the plan is, but it sounds like a good one."

So, he picked up his ol' sack and headed toward the river, and when he got to within half a mile of the river, he heard it. "Here he comes. Here he comes. Here he comes." And he commenced to dying.

"Ooooohhh! Ooooohhhh!" He fell on his back and kicked his legs up in the air.

Well, the sun came out and it was *hot*. It shined directly down on Br'er Coon. He wanted so much to roll up under a shade tree, but Br'er Rabbit had told him not to move, so he just lay there and took it. After a while, the flies came, sat down on his face, crawled in and out of his ears, walked up his nose, and sure enough, he really wanted to move. But he didn't. He just lay there. Finally the sun set, and the flies flew off.

Down through the woods came Br'er Rabbit. He looked out to see if the frogs were there, and there they were, a-waitin'. Br'er Rabbit stood on the edge of the river and commenced to crying.

The bullfrog climbed up on the bank, looked at Br'er Rabbit, and said, "What's the matter with you? What's the matter with you? What's the matter with yoooooou?"

The little frogs said, "What's the matter with

you? What's the matter with you? What's the matter with you?"

Br'er Rabbit said, "Oooooooohhhh, don't you know? My best friend here done fell dead. He done fell dead. Br'er Coon is dead, dead, deeaaad."

The bullfrog said, "Good, good, goooooood."

The little frogs said, "That be good. That be good. That be good."

Br'er Rabbit said, "I promised my friend here years ago that when he passed away I was gonna dig him a grave right here at the place he loved the best. I was gonna dig him a grave right here, right here on the river. Gonna dig it right heeeeeeere."

The bullfrog said, "Let us dig it. Let us dig it. Let *us* dig it."

The little frogs said, "Let us dig it. Let us dig it. Let *us* dig it."

Br'er Rabbit said, "Well, seein' as how I'm so tore up with grief and all, I'm goin' to let you dig it. But I'm goin' to stand right back here under this tree and tell you how deep to dig the grave."

Well sir, the frogs were all gathered around Br'er Coon, and they got out their frog shovels and commenced to dig. It was a curious sight. Br'er Coon was layin' there dead, the frogs was a-diggin' his grave right from under him, and Br'er Rabbit was standin' out under the tree a-watchin'.

The grave got deeper and deeper. As Br'er Coon went down in the grave, the frogs went down in the grave with him. The dirt was flyin'.

The grave was seven feet deep and the frogs was still a-diggin'. The bullfrog thought that that was enough.

Leapin' upon Br'er Coon's chest, he hollered up to Br'er Rabbit. "Is it deep enough? Is it deep enough? Is it deeeeeep enough?"

The little frogs said, "Is it deep enough? Is it deep enough? Is it deep enough?"

Br'er Rabbit ran over to the grave and said, "Well, can you jump out?"

And the bullfrog looked up to see. "Yes, we can. Yes, we can. *Yes*, we can."

The little frogs said, "Yes, we can. Yes, we can. Yes, we can."

Br'er Rabbit said, "Well, it ain't deep enough. Dig it deeper."

The frogs was a-gettin' mighty tired, but they kept a-diggin'. They dug and they dug. The grave was twelve feet deep, and the frogs was still a-diggin'. The bullfrog thought that that was enough.

He leaped upon Br'er Coon's chest and hollered up out of the grave. "Is it deep enough? Is it deep enough? Is it deeeeeeep enough?"

The little frogs said, "Is it deep enough? Is it deep enough? Is it deep enough?"

Br'er Rabbit said, "Well, can you jump out?"

And the bullfrog looked up to see. "Believe we can. Believe we can. *Believe* we can."

The little frogs said, "Believe we can. Believe we can. Believe we can."

Br'er Rabbit said, "It ain't deep enough. Dig it deeper."

Well, the frogs kept a-diggin'. They were mighty tired. Their little old legs were gettin' weak. They commenced to lay down all over Br'er Coon. Br'er Coon started to turn a little green, but he stayed still and never moved. The bullfrog thought that that was enough. The grave was twenty feet deep.

The bullfrog leaped upon Br'er Coon's head, looked up, and said, "Is it deep enough? Is it deep enough? Is it deeeeeeep enough?"

The little frogs said, "Is it deep enough? Is it deep enough? Is it deep enough?"

Br'er Rabbit said, "Well, can you jump out?"

The bullfrog looked up to see. "No, we can't. No, we can't. *No*, we can't."

The little frogs said, "No, we can't. No, we can't. No, we can't."

Br'er Rabbit said, "Get up there, Br'er Coon, and grab your groceries. They're too tired to jump out of the hole."

And ol' Br'er Coon had enough frogs to do him that year and the next year, too.

THIS IS NOWHERE NEAR THE END OF MY LIFE. I have had many adventures since those years have passed.

I offer these reminiscences to my readers in hope that you too will look at your own life—past the agitation, confusion, trauma, and stagnation—and pick out something that was worth remembering in your past. My memories were therapeutic. Here's hoping yours will be, too. ❧